WHAT PEOPLE ARE SAYING ABOUT VOICES 2

Apostle Robert Gay is a credible, experienced, and educated prophetic minister to the body of Christ today. He is a family man who is dedicated to dispensing biblical truth to this generation as well as those to come. Based on over 40 years of ministry leadership and loving dedication to the truth pertaining to the teachings of Jesus Christ, he has shared important insights and advice regarding how to navigate through the plethora of voices who claim to speak for Jesus today. Volume 2 of the *Voices Trilogy* will not tickle ears but will provide a roadmap on the parameters of discerning which of the voices speaking to us today are speaking for Jesus as measured by our Lord's own words.—PASTOR JAY MCKESEY, NEW VISION CHRISTIAN CENTER, ORLANDO, FL

Perhaps one of the greatest needs we have as the people of God while living in such "dangerous times" is for crystal clear discernment. In *Voices 2*, apostolic leader Robert Gay sounds the clarion call of prophetic warning to guard our hearts and minds as never before. From the inception of original sin in Eden, God asks Adam the loaded question, "*Who told you that...?*" We are likewise faced with the same dilemma in the modern world. Where are we gathering our information? And who can we trust? The Word of God is supposed to be the absolute final authority in the life of a Christ-follower; yet, so many seem confused about navigating a godless culture, even questioning some of the most basic principles of life. This book is a deep dive into the quagmire of deception yet infuses the reader with the antidote: the grace and truth of a loving Savior, Jesus the Christ. Thanks to Robert Gay, the fraudulent spirit of this age has no place left to hide!—DR. RICHARD K. PERINCHIEF, SENIOR PASTOR/FOUNDER OF NOW CHURCH, OCALA, FL

Every person who has a desire to hear God's voice clearly should read this book. Pastor Robert writes a masterpiece—this teaching doesn't have a price tag. You need this in your life RIGHT NOW. I will teach from these principles for decades to come. Integrity is being restored to the prophetic movement, and this book is the tip of the spear.— PASTOR COLE BURKS, HOPE UNLIMITED CHURCH, KNOXVILLE, TN

When virtually every safeguard and protocol for sound prophetic ministry has been violated in the most egregious ways, we desperately need a voice that demands we remember from whence we have fallen and then calls us to repentance. Thank God for Pastor Robert Gay and this second installment of his *Voices* trilogy. This book is the straightforward reckoning we need, a calling to account that is at once both humble and bold, holding within its pages hope and direction to help us correct our errors and restore integrity to the beautiful gift that is prophecy. Paul implores us to discern the voices we hear in the Church by proving all things, holding fast to what is right, and shunning every hint of evil. Pastor Robert's voice has been proven time and time again as one of wisdom and revelation. This book is a guiding light, helping us recover our pure, Spirit-inspired utterance that can speak truth to power, deliver the captive, and proclaim the Good News. May God use this work to drive away the noise where nothing is left but His still small voice.—PASTOR CASEY DOSS, THE RAMP SCHOOL OF MINISTRY, HAMILTON, AL

Once again, Pastor Robert Gay has written an anointed and insightful book, which deals with the much-needed truths concerning the voices we allow in our lives. I absolutely love the book. For those who want to stay on a clear path of truth and discernment, I earnestly recommend this material for spiritual growth. It provides clarity in the midst of a world of confusion and chaos and practical steps to discern which voices one may be listening to. Don't just read the book; get one for a friend, for we all need to be sure that we are heeding the correct voices that JESUS has put in our lives and not those of the enemy. You will be richly and immensely blessed as you let these words penetrate your heart and mind.—PASTOR TODD BEAL, NEW & LIVING WAY CHURCH, KELSO, WA

In *Voices 2*, Robert Gay exposes the deceptive traps of the enemy that seek to contaminate the purity of our voice but also skillfully communicates the wisdom needed to walk out our salvation with fear and trembling. While reading, I became very aware of Robert's motivation to challenge the reader to use their gifts and platforms of influence to represent the purity of the Father's love. Robert writes, "It is good to take a stand for righteousness, but it is not right to become the voice of condemnation." *Voices 2* is a relevant must-read!—DR. MELODYE HILTON, LEADERSHIP CONSULTANT/MASTER EXECUTIVE COACH & PASTOR OF GIVING LIGHT CHURCH, ELIZABETHVILLE, PA

2

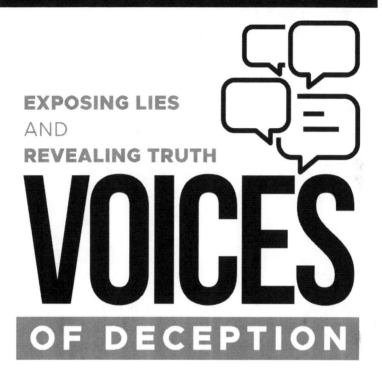

EXPOSING LIES
AND
REVEALING TRUTH

VOICES

OF DECEPTION

DR. ROBERT GAY

Melbourne, Florida USA

Voices of Deception—Exposing Lies and Revealing Truth
by Robert Gay

With a Foreword by Dr. Joseph Mattera.

Parsons Publishing House
P. O. Box 410063
Melbourne, FL 32940 USA
www.ParsonsPublishingHouse.com
Info@ParsonsPublishingHouse.com

Book 2 of The Voices Trilogy by Dr. Robert Gay.

Cover Art by Micah Gay.

DEDICATION

This book is dedicated to all the pastors and leaders who have been faithful to the Lord, their families, the Church, and the Word of God.

During the last several years (2020 til present), ministers have had opportunities to get off course and follow roads that compromised their integrity, call, and purpose. Unfortunately, some have succumbed to the allure that has been present. In the face of the many challenges, many church leaders have resigned and sought different vocations, yet many have been resilient and stood strong.

For all that have stayed the course, I commend you. Well done, and continue your pursuit of the Lord.

VOICES 2

TABLE OF CONTENTS

VOICES 2

FOREWORD

by Dr. Joseph Mattera
Overseeing Bishop of Christ Covenant Coalition

Deception is the hardest thing to uncover due to the nature of its existence. A person experiencing deception is not aware of their deception because if they were, they would not be deceived!

While many in the charismatic movement are running around looking for personal prophetic words, they neglect what's needed even more—biblical discernment.

Scripture teaches us that discernment doesn't come overnight; it develops over time through a lifestyle of practicing spiritual disciplines. These include the study of Scripture, worship, submission to spiritual authority, participating in the life of a local church, sitting under biblical teaching, and having a robust prayer life so a person can learn how to hear the voice of God (see Hebrews 5:11-14).

Hence, it's much easier to go to a conference for a prophetic word than to discipline oneself to seek the Lord regularly. Only His Word can shape your worldview and develop your character.

The book of Proverbs teaches us, "The integrity of the upright guides them, but the crookedness of the treacherous destroys them... The righteousness of the blameless keeps his way straight, but the wicked falls by his own wickedness" (Proverbs 11:3, 5, ESV). Consequently, it is not just receiving the gift of prophecy and attempting to hear the voice of God in our spirits. Spiritual formation that develops godly character to matriculate us toward discernment grants us the capacity to discern the difference between right and wrong.

The apostle Paul told Titus, "To the pure, all things are pure, but to the defiled and unbelieving, nothing is pure; but both their minds and their consciences are defiled" (Titus 1:15, ESV). That is to say, if our heart is duplicitous and defiled, our worldview will be defiled, our hearts will be dull, and we will be unable to distinguish between right and wrong, resulting in a profound lack of discernment.

All of this is not easy to hear for the quick-fix microwave generation of charismatics who depend solely upon receiving prophetic words, angelic visitations, visions, and dreams as a guide for their lives. Although these modes of supernatural communication are still valid today, they were never meant to replace a life of discipline that centers itself around seeking the Lord and living in the context of godly Christ-followers. There is also something to be said about the importance of doing life together with other Christ-followers in a local church that enables us to hear what the Spirit is saying to the church (Revelation 2:7). It is also not a coincidence that Jesus called His followers "disciples" and brought them into a community centered around Him.

The word "disciple" implies focus and a life of discipline. However, it was not merely individual discipline but discipline in the context of having a right relationship with other disciples that helped frame their view of the Master, who prepared them to be His witnesses to the ends of the earth (Acts 1:8-9).

Thus, in the context of personal discipline, living in a Christ-focused community with Jesus as Lord developed a life of discernment for the first-century apostles so that when Jesus ascended into heaven, they were ready to start the greatest movement the world has ever seen. It was only in community that they were able to learn from one another—test their basic assumptions, put the Word into practice, and discern the difference between true faith, delusion, and demonic deception.

In this book which is the second part in a series on voices, my dear friend Robert Gay culls his experience as a practitioner for over four decades—functioning as a nationally known worship leader, prophet, and leader who established a significant apostolic church.

He elaborates on various levels and expressions of deception common today that only a seasoned shepherd/prophet would be able to discern and utilize to bless the body of Christ.

I always enjoy listening to his teaching, his insights, and reading his books. He is an amazing gift to the body of Christ for such a time as this!

VOICES 2

INTRODUCTION

In the world today, many different voices are being heralded from every direction. We hear the voices of our friends and families. There are voices we hear at our local church from fellow members of the body of Christ. We also listen to voices from leadership positions charged with correctly guiding those in their care. All these voices are unique and promote varied narratives that are broadcast by each.

We also experience internal voices. Since we are a spirit, have a soul, and live in a body, we must discern every voice of our trichotomy. Each part of our makeup has a voice and must be processed correctly. As Christians, we can hear the voice of the Holy Spirit as He leads and guides us on the path of life. These internal and external voices must be sifted through every day.

There are also the voices we hear in the various forms of media and entertainment. We listen to them on television and radio with their particular viewpoints and perspectives concerning everything under the sun. One will say something only to be followed by a different voice declaring something contrary. There can be many variations of what they individually claim as truth according to the slant applied to what they speak and the viewership to whom they appeal. But, of course, we know none of them could ever say something false, right?

Social media has given rise to platforms for people who know little about anything. However, through appeal mechanisms, they garner followers who are influenced by their voice. Many people follow these voices because they like what they hear. It agrees with a predisposition they support or becomes a mob flow in which they are captured.

It seems we are constantly swimming in a sea of voices coming from every direction and place with a constant introduction of new voices. Yet, each claims to be the bearer of truth, and it becomes impossible to block them all.

Defining Truth

At the end of the day, we are tasked with the job of discerning all these voices. We must evaluate and determine which ones are accurate and which ones are false. We must distinguish the voice of truth from the voice of deception.

It appears that truth is now being redefined by many as merely what they want it to be and what they want to hear. In some minds, facts and evidence mean very little. Predisposed opinions and desires have taken a front seat to what these people declare as the truth. Unfortunately, those who embrace this form of truth analysis are the first people to become victims of the voices of deception.

When voices contradict one another, it becomes apparent that something is amiss. The contradiction leaves those who hear these voices with the choice of what they will embrace or reject. It is a choice we make every day, and most people are not conscious of it because it is typically done automatically based on opinions, positions, understandings, or biases they may already possess.

We must understand that a voice does not speak the truth solely because it has a platform from which to speak. Platforms never indicate the truthfulness of a voice. Lies are constantly uttered from various platforms, specifically those with underlying goals of garnering or placating an audience. These voices will typically spin the truth into something appealing to their followers. Some who hear these augmentations will say, *"This is the truth!"* while not realizing they are being manipulated into believing something that is false and deceptive. It happens every day we live, both in spiritual and natural matters.

The Slant Fosters Deception

Not long ago, I was at home watching the news of a major world crisis, with continual coverage broadcasting on all major news networks. So, I decided to give a short listen to hear what was being said. Not surprisingly, every news outlet shared the same story with a distinct perspective and viewpoint.

Some reports were remarkably similar and had little editorialization. However, the news agencies that augmented the story through imposed opinions seemed to speak different languages. It was as if they were reporting on opposing stories; the difference in reporting the "truth" from these outlets was amazing. These contradictory stories were not merely a unique perspective of the truth. They were narratives riddled with editorialization that skewed the truth into a storyline exclusively designed to make their viewers happy. As a result, the "truth" was lost and buried in the spin and slant of the story. The news media is only one of the many places where this regularly happens.

Believing the Lie Brings Deception

In my first book in this series, entitled *Voices*, I share how the Holy Spirit enables Christians to discern the voices we hear. This book will focus on different voices of deception the enemy uses to manipulate people. Satan uses these voices to defraud believers of their spiritual inheritance in Christ Jesus. These are the voices the devil exploits to sow seeds of discord and division in the body of Christ. These are also the voices that satan employs to keep unbelievers blind to the truth.

Voices of deception are extremely dangerous to Christians when they go undiscerned. What makes these voices so harmful is those who believe them think their source is the possessor of truth. The ones being deceived are not necessarily evil in heart and motive; they merely believe the wrong thing. They believe a lie and call it the truth. They believe something false while shouting, *"The truth will set you free!"*

It Happened in the Beginning

In the very beginning of time, as we know it, a specific pattern can be seen that unfortunately still happens today. In Genesis 1, we witness the creation of the world in which we live. God created a perfect environment for man to abide and thrive. Along with this, He gave man a mission to fulfill with the tools to get the job done.

In Genesis 2, we witness the creation of woman, the Garden of Eden, and a responsibility placed in the hands of man. Adam was given a specific job with a helper to accomplish the task. God set everything in order so that man could succeed in his mission. A perfect environment was established for a perfect man and woman to be a perfect team and have a perfect home and family while accomplishing God's perfect plan for their lives.

In Genesis 3, everything goes south. The serpent deceives Eve while Adam watches the whole thing go down. He willfully sins and partakes of the forbidden fruit as the entire world is sent into a catastrophic spin. The place of perfection becomes a place of pain and shame. Everything Adam and Eve received was forfeited in one moment.

This is a pattern that seems to repeat itself all too frequently. People are given a divine purpose when they are saved. They are given the tools to accomplish God's call upon their lives. God places them in an environment to succeed and prosper. However, they listen to the wrong voice at some point and end up forfeiting it all.

All the sin in the world today is due to someone falling prey to the voice of deception. Eve was deceived by the serpent and disobeyed God. I do not believe she possessed a heart bent toward evil, but her deception ultimately resulted in her being removed from their home in the garden. The serpent deceived her and plunged all humanity into sin.

The serpent was given a platform—the Garden of Eden combined with man's curiosity. His familiar voice made Eve willing to hear it. Adam listened to the voice of his wife, Eve, possibly because he trusted her. However, their lack of ability to discern properly caused them both to sin. Their transgression resulted in them losing everything. We will discuss this in greater detail later in this writing.

The problems and calamities that people encounter in the world today can usually be traced back to someone giving their ear to the voice of deception. People do sinful and ungodly things while believing they are justified in their actions. This dynamic happens in every realm of life due to people being deceived. The voice of deception causes good people to do dreadful things.

Saying Evil Is Good

In my 40 years of ministry, I have witnessed some people do incredibly bad things. Yet, as sinful as some of these things were, the worst thing they did was to justify themselves after the fact. It is one thing to do evil, yet doubly bad to say that an evil committed is good. This paradox happens when voices of deception are given place within someone's life.

Unfortunately, this happens to both unbelievers and Christians. We must understand that being born-again does not alone protect a Christian from voices of deception. Believers must fortify themselves through the Word of God, the work of the Holy Spirit, and a strong spiritual covering to prevent falling under the spell of these lying voices.

Being saved and filled with the Holy Spirit will not by itself keep someone from being deceived. As wonderful as it is to pray in the Spirit, it will not alone prevent someone from succumbing to these voices with destructive intent. It is my prayer that you will properly discern these voices that come to defraud people of their spiritual inheritance.

Turn on the Light

Not long ago, I got up in the middle of the night. The darkness prevented me from seeing where I was walking, and as a result, I stumped my toe. It hurt so bad that I began to hop on one foot and fell back into the bed. My wife asked what happened, and I told her about stumping my toe on the doorframe. She replied, *"You need to turn on the light!"* She was right.

This accident resulted in my toe and the surrounding area of my foot turning black and blue; it was probably broken. I had difficulty walking for several weeks, and it hurt even to put a shoe on my foot. Throughout the healing process, the pain prevented me from doing many ordinary tasks. It could have all been avoided if I had turned on the light. Instead, walking in the dark caused me to hurt myself unintentionally.

The purpose of this book is to turn on the spiritual light. Many Christians are stumping their toe and experiencing pain solely because they are unaware that they are listening to voices of deception. It negatively impacts their lives, and they end up incapacitated, hopping around on one foot. This needlessly happens because many people are walking in the dark and cannot recognize the voices of deception whispering in their ears.

I believe as you read this book, the Holy Spirit will illuminate truth to your heart. I believe the light will shine and reveal these voices that come to steal, kill, and destroy. The voices that seek to bring a forfeiture of God's purpose for your life will be silenced as you embrace the light of the truth. Allow the Lord to do this in your life.

VOICES 2

1

DECEPTION HAS A VOICE

Now the serpent was more cunning than any beast of the field which the LORD God had made. And he said to the woman, "Has God indeed said, 'You shall not eat of every tree of the garden'?" And the woman said to the serpent, "We may eat the fruit of the trees of the garden; but of the fruit of the tree which is in the midst of the garden, God has said, 'You shall not eat it, nor shall you touch it, lest you die.'" Then the serpent said to the woman, "You will not surely die. For God knows that in the day you eat of it your eyes will be opened, and you will be like God, knowing good and evil." So when the woman saw that the tree was good for food, that it was pleasant to the eyes, and a tree desirable to make one wise, she took of its fruit and ate. She also gave to her husband with her, and he ate. Then the eyes of both of them were opened, and they knew that they were naked; and they sewed fig leaves together and made themselves coverings. And they heard the sound of the LORD God walking in the garden in the cool of the day, and Adam

and his wife hid themselves from the presence
of the LORD God among the trees of the
garden (Genesis 3:1-8).

At the very beginning of human existence, God created an environment of perfection for man to inhabit. He planted a garden, placed man in it, and then gave him the responsibility of tending it. Along with this, God created a mate—helper—spouse for Adam, and her name was Eve. She was God's crowning achievement since she was the last of His earthly creations. While man was refined from the earth, she was refined from man. She was twice-refined.

Eve's responsibility was to help Adam. God created her because He saw that it was not good for man to be alone. He needed another human being that would be different yet qualify as his partner. So, in God's wisdom, He created a masterpiece that completed Adam and gave him everything needed to accomplish his purpose. Man and woman were united to take dominion on the earth as equal heirs of the grace of God.

We do not know exactly how long Adam and Eve were in the garden before the serpent showed up to tempt them. It could have been one day or thousands of years. We have no idea and could only speculate. However, it is reasonable to say that Adam and Eve were fulfilling their purpose together for a time. It is equally reasonable to say that this was not the serpent's first trip to the garden, where he most likely lived and dwelled since it was a food source.

Satan's Tactics Seen

By studying this account, we can see the tools and tactics of satan. It is important to understand that the devil does not have any new techniques. Strategies he practiced from the beginning are the same ones he uses today. The same devil uses the same thing on different people with different faces. Unfortunately, people continue to fall prey to the same things that captured Adam and Eve in the beginning.

Many theologians have different opinions on the serpent that we will not discuss in this writing. However, we know that the serpent's voice was the voice of the deceiver; it was the voice of our enemy, satan. It was the voice of the thief desiring to steal, kill, and destroy. It was the voice of the destroyer.

When Eve heard the serpent's voice, she had the chance to say "*No!*" and correct him quickly. She had the opportunity at that very moment to tell the serpent his assumption of God defrauding them of wisdom was wrong. However, instead of hearing the voice of the serpent as a thief and robber, she heard it as a friend and helper. As a result, Eve sinned by eating the fruit of the forbidden tree.

Adam, who was standing by her at the time, ate also. This act opened the door for all humanity to be controlled by the law of sin and death. The entire earth launched into a cataclysmic shift as death entered the place where only life could previously exist. This shift was the result of sin and disobedience.

Failure to Discern Produced Sin

The introduction of sin into the earth was rooted in Eve's failure to discern the voice she was hearing. She perceived the serpent's voice as one that could help her. Eve believed that listening to him had the potential to make her wiser. His voice was soothing to her soul and promised what she recognized was needed in her life: knowledge and wisdom.

Believing that the voice of the serpent had the ability to further her purpose and make her wiser (even though it only had the power to do the opposite) caused her to fall into sin. Her error was rooted in the inability to discern that she was listening to the voice of one who sought to steal and destroy. She believed that she was hearing the voice of a promise keeper when in fact, she was listening to a liar.

The Familiar Voice

Far too often, Christians make decisions based on natural voices they hear. It may come from their friend, relative, coworker, neighbor, or any other familiar person. They believe the voice they hear speaks truth and will not lead them astray. However, hearing the voice of a friend does not guarantee that what they are saying is the counsel one needs. We must be able to discern what is right and wrong, godly and ungodly, spiritual and fleshly, along with truthful and false.

Think about this for a moment. Adam and Eve lost their home, food supply, and fellowship with God in one moment because of improper discernment. They were removed from paradise on earth because of believing the voice of the thief was the voice of the helper. When they exited the garden, the only thing they possessed was some souvenir clothing that God made for them.

Unfortunately, many people today end up forfeiting God's best for their lives because they heed the wrong voices. They perceive the voice of the enemy as the voice of a friend. Sometimes the enemy's voice may even be articulated through their friend. Yet, because they cannot properly discern the voice, they fall into the snare of the enemy. Instead of receiving the fullness of God's blessing, they must settle with the souvenir of a partial blessing equivalent to a piece of clothing. Having clothing is better than walking around naked but is still far beneath God's best for anyone's life.

Believing Something Is True When It Is Not

It is apparent that Eve's actions violated the command given to her. She disobeyed God, as did her husband, Adam. However, I believe Eve was convinced she was doing something good that could enlighten her when she partook of the fruit. She believed this would empower the purpose God created for them to fulfill together.

Paul specifically said that Eve was deceived:

> "For Adam was first formed, then Eve. And Adam was not
> deceived, but the woman being deceived was in the
> transgression" (1 Timothy 2:13-14).

To be deceived means that you do something with a false understanding in your mind. When someone is deceived, it does not mean they are necessarily evil in their intent. It means their intent is corrupted by incorrect information and perception.

The definition of the word "deceive" is to *cause someone to believe something that is not true.* Further, it means *to cause to accept as true or valid what is false or invalid.* Synonyms for this word are swindle, defraud, cheat, trick, or hoodwink. The truth is that someone who is deceived becomes the victim of the deceiver.

The previous verse of Scripture makes it apparent that Eve was deceived, yet Adam sinned willfully as he failed to protect his wife from the voice of the deceiver. Adam was standing by his wife when the dialogue with the serpent was ongoing yet did nothing to prevent the downward spiral. It appears he wanted to see what would happen to her before he ate the fruit himself. As a result of his passivity and disengagement, Eve became victimized by satan as she was deceived by the voice of the serpent.

When people are deceived, they become victims of the power behind the voices to which they are listening. They believe they are hearing correctly, doing the right thing, and following the truth. However, they have only been sold a bag of goods that later proves false. It is difficult for someone to embrace the truth when they are deceived by a lie; they believe the lie they heard is the truth.

The Devil Is a Liar

> You are of your father the devil, and the desires of your father you want to do. He was a murderer from the beginning, and does not stand in the truth, because there is no truth in him. When he speaks a lie, he speaks from his own resources, for he is a liar and the father of it (John 8:44).

Jesus said that satan is a liar. He went on to say that the devil is the father of lies, which means that he is the originator of all lies, untruths, and deceptions. The only thing that the enemy can do is lie. He has no ability to speak the truth because it is not within him. Therefore, it is impossible for him to utter anything correctly.

We observe this happening with Eve in the beginning. The serpent told her, "You will not surely die." He further expanded the lie to say that she would be like God. Wow, that is significantly different from what God initially told Adam and Eve.

The truth was that eating the fruit did cause her to die. Partaking of the fruit caused her to become separated from God. Furthermore, Eve's act of disobedience caused her to cease being like God any longer. The results were the exact opposite of everything the serpent told her. Eve was deceived, and Adam went along with the entire ordeal. Their actions ended with losing everything that God had magnificently provided for them.

The Lure and Enticement of Deception

Deceptions are rooted in lies. The voice of the enemy will utter twisted truth that is fallacious at its core. These lies are the basis and foundation where deception gets its foothold. The serpent twisted the truth that God spoke to Adam and Eve so he could deceive them. The devil made his appeal attractive, believable, and acceptable.

For someone to be deceived by a voice, there must be some element of perceived truth and positive enticement. There will usually be a measure of truth in the statement of deception to make it believable. If it is not plausible, then no one could be deceived. If the voice did not promise something good and desirable, it could not persuade anyone to follow its invitation.

There will usually be just enough truth in the voice of deception to persuade an individual that the lie is the truth. If it was evident that the voice was lying, it could find no place within the heart of someone. Deception is a lie perceived as truth.

When someone walks in deception, it is very difficult to reason with them. They are not easily removed from what they believe, even when false. You can speak with them and show them the truth that contradicts the voice of deception, but they will cling to the lie like a starving man to a morsel of bread. These people take a heart disposition that refuses to be moved or changed by the voice of reason or proof.

Those who fall prey to the voice of deception believe they are right, which is what makes it so heinous. They are thoroughly convinced that they are holders and bearers of the truth. Their belief is that they have seen the light and everyone else is in darkness. This is how false religions and cults gain control over individuals; it is through the voice of deception.

Everything Good is Not God

We must understand that everything that sounds good is not from God, everything that glitters is not gold, and everything that smells good should not be eaten. It is dangerous for anyone to evaluate something purely by what is perceived externally. Christians must learn to discern by the spirit, both our recreated human spirit and the Holy Spirit. Failure to do this will result in someone following and going after things that appear godly on the surface yet are not at the core.

This same thing happened with Eve. The voice of the serpent presented something that appeared great on the surface. He said that her eyes would be opened, and she would be like God. Is there anyone who would not want that? These are great things to possess. The enemy used a promise of something godly to cause Eve to do something ungodly. He deceived her with his lie.

Empowered by a False Motivation

One thing that gives the voice of deception power is the belief that it is godly motivated. It is the conviction that complete truth is contained within that which is utterly false. This belief causes people to become passionate about the lie that they believe. They become indignant if anyone challenges them with actual truth. Many times, their lives become so intertwined with the deception that it is difficult for them to separate it from their own identity. These are the most dangerous forms of lies and deception.

For these people to recant the deception, they believe it would require a total deconstruction of themselves. The reason for this is the deception wraps itself around their personage. Those who are controlled by this degree of deception need spiritual deliverance. They need to be transformed by the renewing of their mind.

The voice of the enemy will promise you the moon and fail to deliver a piece of a fallen asteroid. His lie will give you rational justification for doing things that are sinful yet only result in a journey down the road of unrighteousness. The voice of deception will promise the very things you have always desired but will only produce the undesirable within your life. Therefore, we must crush the lies and deception of the enemy with true and accurate spiritual discernment.

The Spiritual Weapon of Truth

Jesus said, "I am the way, the truth, and the life" (John 14:6). He is the truth in full manifestation. He can only speak and utter the truth. Anything that is contrary to what Jesus said is a lie. If Jesus said it, then it is the truth. While it may not be in manifestation or existence within your life at present, it is still the truth because He uttered it. This is a foundation upon which our lives must be established, or we will live with open ears to the voice of deception.

The greatest way to discern and ward off the enemy's voice is with truth. It is the best weapon to combat the onslaught of the devil; truth has the power and authority to expose the lie and crush the voice of deception. In speaking about the armor of God, the apostle Paul instructed believers to have their loins girded with truth. This protects Christians from the lies of hell.

The very first place we should look to establish truth is in the words of Jesus. His Word is the primary weapon to be used against the voice of deception. If you hear things contrary to what Jesus said, it must be deemed false.

Know the Bible

Much deception can be cut off immediately just by having knowledge of the words of Jesus. There are so many Christians today who have never studied the Gospels. They talk about preaching the gospel but have failed to read and study the first four books of the New Testament. We will have a tough time preaching the gospel if we fail to possess any knowledge of what Jesus said.

Unfortunately, many Christians are biblically illiterate. They will declare that Jesus said things that He never spoke while being ignorant of what He repeatedly said. This ignorance is one of the things that has given power to the voice of deception. It has enabled the lies of the enemy to take root in many who claim to be Christians resulting in believers not acting in a Christlike manner. Instead, they continue practicing their old lifestyle filled with ungodliness, malice, and hatred.

These are things that need to change in the body of Christ. We must begin to gain knowledge of the words of Jesus. It is His words that become the weapons we use to ward off and crush the lies of hell. It enables us to properly discern voices filled with deception and then avoid their influence.

Jesus, Our Example

When the devil tempted Jesus, He overcame every lie and deception the enemy used by quoting Scripture. When enticed to make bread out of stones, Jesus said, "It is written, 'Man shall not live by bread alone, but by every word that proceeds from the mouth of God'" (Matthew 4:4). With every temptation and deception of satan, Jesus combated it with "It is written." He overcame the deceiver with the Word of God.

Jesus left an example for all believers to follow. The voice of deception should always be met with the words He spoke, which disables the enemy's tactics within the life of a Christian. Contrastingly, ignorance of the Word empowers the voice of the enemy in one's life. Someone is open game when they lack knowledge of the words of Jesus. **It is impossible to *speak* the Word if you do not *know* the Word. Think about it!**

The only thing the devil can do is lie; he is incapable of speaking the truth. He will mask his lies by twisting and distorting the truth, hoping people will unknowingly believe the lie he propagates while believing they are embracing the truth. Those who do not know the truth of the Word will ultimately fall prey to the lies satan seeks to advance. These are the reasons that knowledge of God's Word is so crucial today. We must know the truth to combat the voice of deception.

Ears That Need Scratching

There are more voices on the earth than at any time we have previously known. With the internet and social media advancements, there has come an onslaught of lies and falsehoods. We are bombarded daily with posts, blogs, and articles that seem to utter truth on the surface, yet they are found to have numerous contradictions when researched. Many of them are blatant lies and rumors that appeal to a particular group; it feeds what they desire to be true. Somewhere on the internet, there is an article, post, blog, or video available to articulate anything one wants to think or believe.

Numerous internet postings are wrapped with the spiritual bow of a Scripture yet convey a message that is not entirely truthful. Unfortunately, some Christians unknowingly embrace the message because of the bow on the package. It sounds like the Word, yet they cannot discern the error contained in it.

> Preach the word! Be ready in season and out of season. Convince, rebuke, exhort, with all longsuffering and teaching. For the time will come when they will not endure sound doctrine, but according to their own desires,

because they have itching ears, they will heap
up for themselves teachers; and they will turn
their ears away from the truth, and be turned
aside to fables (2 Timothy 4:2-4).

There are many things that can be derived from this passage of
Scripture that we will unpack in chapter five. First, focus your
attention on what Paul said in verse three. He said, "but
according to their own desires, because they have itching ears,
they will heap up for themselves teachers." He mentions a
common problem in the Church today, that of "itching ears."
People have an itch they want to be scratched. They possess an
idea or belief that they want to be confirmed as the truth, even
though it may be totally false. Having someone say what they
want to hear makes them feel consoled and then justified in
their view and perspective. This danger zone is where the voice
of deception has the opportunity of taking advantage of
believers.

Unfortunately, this behavior is leading the Church down a path
where it looks less and less like Jesus. Believers do things that
are not Christlike while shouting the name of Jesus at the same
time. They lift up banners to identify themselves as believers,
yet their actions are everything except what Jesus would do. At
the root of these things is the voice of deception. This must
change in the body of Christ.

Turning from the Truth

Paul went on to say in this passage that these teachers and
proclaimers would "turn their ears away from the truth." He is
referring to Christians being deceived because they want to
hear a particular thing stated as the truth even though it is false.

The itch they want to have scratched is stronger than their desire for the truth of God's Word and the voice of the Holy Spirit. They want their belief to be confirmed and declared accurate, while they believe nothing more than a fable. They refuse the truth because it is not what they want to hear. My friend, this is a dangerous place to be.

It is exceedingly difficult to turn people in the right direction when they get to this point because their ears have been turned away from the truth. The truth is difficult to hear when one's ears turn to something else. When someone's hearing is turned, they will not hear correctly. Words of correction will seem like words of condemnation. The voice of truth will seem like the voice of falsehood. The voice of reason will sound like the voice of babble.

We must understand that the devil does not show up with a red bodysuit, long tail, pitchfork, and shout, *"The devil is here."* He is subtle in his maneuvering. Paul said he would come as an angel of light and illumination; he conceals his identity. So likewise, the voice of deception conceals its identity. It will not be obvious; it is subtle and contains just enough truth to make itself believable.

The Doorway for Deception

I believe it is very possible that Eve wanted to hear someone say, *"It's ok for you to eat of the tree, go ahead."* There had to be a starting place in Eve's heart for this temptation to find a home. The voice of deception found an open door where it could enter. **Is it possible that Adam and Eve had an itch they wanted to be scratched, and the voice of deception was able to accommodate them? Think about it.**

In the forty years of my own personal ministry, I have found that temptation and deception can find no entry into someone's life unless they already possess a propensity to engage in some sort of sinful behavior. For example, someone who has no desire to be famous cannot be tempted by fame. Someone who has no desire to be wealthy cannot be tempted with the pursuit of money. A person with no desire to have a sexual relationship with someone other than their spouse cannot be tempted with adultery. The problem exists in the itch that people want scratched, which gives the voice of deception potential power in both believers and unbelievers.

The doorway for the voice of deception is the itch that many want to be scratched. It is the strong bias from which one may approach the Word of God that causes them to see through tinted glasses. The ungodly beliefs within one's life cause perspectives to be skewed, which will cause people to desire to hear specific things even though they may be false. These people study their Bible, hear a sermon, or read an article and come away with something that was never said because they seek to validate a specific message or narrative.

These doorways and avenues that enable the voice of deception to have access must be closed by **the truth of God's Word**, the **voice of the Holy Spirit**, and **strong spiritual discernment**. These three things activated within the life of a Christian will alleviate the itching ears that many possess. The more we rid ourselves of prejudices and biases (both spiritual and natural), the more we close the door to voices that speak lies. The bottom line is that one is vulnerable to the voice of deception if they possess an itch they want to have scratched.

Preach the Word

At the beginning of the passage of Scripture concerning itching ears, Paul said, "Preach the Word!" He was giving the solution for the issue of people with itching ears. Paul told Timothy to keep preaching the Word. Do not deviate from God's Word. Regardless of public opinions of the day, preach the Word. Regardless of the school of thought and cultural influences of the times, preach the Word. **This message is vital for pastors and leaders to grasp and understand.**

Paul told Timothy to recognize that there would be people with itching ears; however, he should never stoop to the level of scratching their itch. It is Paul who said, "For I am not ashamed of the gospel of Christ, for it is the power of God unto salvation" (Romans 1:16). He was saying the solution is found in the gospel. The answers to problems in our society, culture, and nation are found in the power of the gospel because only the gospel can change the heart of man—a politician cannot. Nothing can transform the hearts and lives of men and women other than the gospel of Jesus Christ.

Some forces and voices will attempt to pressure church leaders to use the pulpit as a place to articulate cultural, political, and societal narratives. However, we must understand that ministry gifts are anointed to preach the gospel; they are ordained to preach the Word. They are not called to preach and proclaim a societal, political, or cultural doctrine that scratches the ears of those that desire it to be said from the pulpit. Therefore, we should avoid using the pulpit as a platform to prop up a specific political candidate or make statements inferring that God is endorsing them. This warning is particularly applicable in a democracy where this type of statement can become a tool of manipulation.

The Church is called to influence every aspect of society, culture, and government, including politics. This influence is to be done through proclaiming the gospel, which is the power of God unto salvation. Transformation in the lives and hearts of people will translate into every other realm of culture and society.

Laws and governments do not have the power to change cultures since they fail to possess the ability to change the heart of man. The gospel and the transforming power of the Holy Spirit are the agents of change for our society, nation, government, and culture. Attempts to do this in any other manner will always fall short.

Many voices within our culture seek a platform. Some seek the platform of our church's pulpits. However, we must remain faithful to preach the Word, not cultural and political ideology. These philosophies can potentially be contaminated with man's ideas and then deceive multitudes. They may pose as the truth while being riddled with thoughts contrary to the truth of God's Word.

A Lesson from History

In the 1930s, a man came into power in the nation of Germany. His name was Adolf Hitler. History reveals that Hitler was supported by much of the Church in Germany. Only a few Church leaders with spiritual discernment spoke out against the things Hitler sought to do. Some of these leaders were arrested, and some were executed.

The Church in Germany was duped into believing that Hitler was the answer God was sending for their plight. As a result, it was not unusual for salutes to Hitler and the Nazi State to be done in church services because much of the German Church was in league with the Nazi Party.

A German pastor named Hermann Gruner said, "The time is fulfilled for the German people of Hitler. It is because of Hitler that Christ, God the helper and redeemer, has become effective among us.... Hitler is the way of the Spirit and the will of God for the German people to enter the Church of Christ." Another pastor put it more succinctly: "Christ has come to us through Adolph Hitler" (*Christianity Today*, https://www.christianitytoday.com/history/people/martyrs/dietrich-bonhoeffer.html).

Pulpits across Germany became a place of political propagation for Hitler's message. The voice of deception was given a place in churches across the nation. Pastors and congregations believed they were doing what was right. They believed that Hitler was their deliverer. They were convinced that he was the savior meant to restore Germany. The Nazi Party platform stated its support for Christianity, and many believers were enthralled. Only a small sect called the Confessing Church vocalized their objections to Naziism and German nationalism.

Hitler declared that he would restore Germany to its greatness and bring the nation back to its original glory. But, as we are now aware, he did everything but that. The Church of Germany became victimized by the voice of deception because they had an itch they wanted someone to scratch. I cannot help but question if the Holocaust would have happened if the Church had not been deceived.

Those who fail to learn from history are bound to make the same mistakes. So, here is the lesson to be learned: **Those occupying pulpits must remain faithful to preaching the Word and exalting the name of Jesus, not political ideology.** It must be closed to the voice of deception. Pastors and leaders should always preach biblical values but not political talking points. There is a difference.

Pastors should refrain from preaching things merely to make people feel good and scratch their ears. We can never yield to the voices that seek a platform to proclaim human ideologies from the pulpit. Doing so will open the door for deception to enter the Church.

Time for Introspection

I believe that the Church needs to take a serious introspective look inside. We need to allow the Holy Spirit to illuminate anything within us that gives place to the voice of deception. To believe that we cannot be deceived just because we are saved means that we are already deceived. The voice of deception preys on both the saved and the unsaved. Therefore, we must allow Holy Spirit discernment to come alive in us and refuse to allow biases and preconceptions to paint inaccurate images on the canvases of our hearts.

If we humble ourselves in the sight of the Lord, He will help and empower us. If we are proud and arrogant in heart, we will surely fall and become victims of deception. Allow the voice of the Lord living in you to guard against the tactics of the devil.

Pray this with me:

Father, cause my spiritual senses to be keen. Help me correctly discern so I will not fall prey to the voice of deception. I renounce unholy biases, preconceptions, and mindsets that can open doors for the enemy. I place my focus on Jesus, the author and finisher of my faith. I acknowledge that He who began a good work in me will be faithful to complete it. In Jesus' name, Amen!

2

My Friend Said...

"If your brother, the son of your mother, your
son or your daughter, the wife of your bosom,
or your friend who is as your own soul, secretly
entices you, saying, 'Let us go and serve other
gods,' which you have not known, neither you
nor your fathers, of the gods of the people
which are all around you, near to you or far off
from you, from one end of the earth to the
other end of the earth, you shall not consent to
him or listen to him, nor shall your eye pity
him, nor shall you spare him or conceal him"
(Deuteronomy 13:6-8).

Anytime the enemy shows up to deceive someone, he does not
announce his plans, intentions, or tactics. Instead, he will show
up through the voice of someone that is considered a friend or
even a family member. His voice will be heard through a
trusted confidant that one has grown to love and appreciate.
The devil never reveals his identity or the hand that he is
playing.

People are deceived because they believe the voice they hear is
speaking the truth. If they knew what they heard was a lie, it

would be quickly discarded. However, the persuasion of a friend's voice causes many people to believe an untruth that ultimately enables them to be defrauded. It happens every day and in every place with Christians and non-Christians alike.

God specifically warned His people not to be enticed by the voices of family and friends, causing them to sin and do wrong. He gave them specific instruction that no voice was ever to be solely trusted based upon relationship. God revealed that it is possible for family and friends to deceive and lead someone astray.

I recognize this is a hard truth to hear. We want to believe that our family and friends would never do anything to deceive us. We desire to believe that their words can be trusted. After all, what kind of world do we live in if we cannot trust their voice? If we cannot believe them, then who can we believe? These things must be balanced in our minds properly, or else we will live as gullible individuals or become skeptical of everyone.

The good news is that the Holy Spirit has come to lead and guide believers. Jesus said that He would lead us into all truth. That means the Holy Spirit will illuminate what is right and wrong, what is true and false, along with what is accurate and inaccurate. He is our Helper and has come to reveal to us these things so we will not be deceived by voices that speak untruthfully.

A Friend Told Me

As I look back on the account of creation and Eve's encounter with the serpent, I have come to several conclusions. The first one is that Eve was familiar to some degree with the serpent. She did not seem surprised or alarmed that she was communicating with a snake. I am not quite sure how the serpent communicated to her, but there does not seem to be any indication that this was something unusual.

Eve's greatest mistake was that she perceived the serpent to be a friend; she did not see him as someone who came to deceive her. She carried on a conversation with the one who had come to steal, kill, and destroy. Eve perceived the voice of the serpent as one of a trusted friend as she allowed it to entice her into sin and wrongdoing.

Here is a truth that all believers need to understand clearly: **The voice of deception can come from the mouth of a trusted individual.** False statements can be declared by someone who says they love Jesus and you. Even the people who are your closest companions can say things that are not truthful, having the potential to defraud you of the blessing of the Lord.

This is not to say that anyone is lying intentionally. Nor is this inferring that people are deliberately attempting to deceive you. However, friendship does not equate to someone speaking the truth.

There is no greater example of this than when Jesus confronted Simon Peter:

> From that time Jesus began to show to His disciples that He must go to Jerusalem, and suffer many things from the elders and chief priests and scribes, and be killed, and be raised

the third day. Then Peter took Him aside and began to rebuke Him, saying, "Far be it from You, Lord; this shall not happen to You!" But He turned and said to Peter, "Get behind Me, Satan! You are an offense to Me, for you are not mindful of the things of God, but the things of men" (Matthew 16:21-23).

Jesus told His disciples the truth of what was to happen to Him, but Peter did not like what He was saying. So, he took Jesus aside in an attempt to correct and straighten Him out. **After Peter's lecture, Jesus called him "satan." Think about it.** Peter is one of Jesus' trusted disciples, and He calls him the devil.

Here we see an example of how someone close to you can still give voice to things that are untruthful. Peter could not fathom how any of the things that Jesus spoke could be true. If Jesus had said that He was going to overthrow the Romans, establish His kingdom, and give each of His disciples a place of rulership in the nation of Israel, Peter would have cheered and said, *"That's right!"* However, Jesus' words did not agree with the Peter's predisposed opinion of how things were supposed to happen. So, he voiced his opposition, and Jesus declared it was the voice of satan—the voice of deception.

Jesus said that one of His closest disciples was moved by the voice of the devil. Let that sink in for a moment. Peter walked and talked with Jesus. He left his fishing business to follow the Lord. He left everything he owned just for the opportunity to be a disciple of the One he believed to be the Messiah; yet, Jesus called him satan.

God's System of Valuation

The reason that Jesus referred to Peter as satan is clearly stated. It was because Peter was mindful of the things of man and not the things of God. He was caught up in the natural and carnal valuations of life. His value system was based on the manner in which man evaluated success. Jesus' system of valuation was spiritual; Peter's was fleshly and carnal. Jesus was governed by heavenly values, while the earthly law of survival governed Peter.

The truth is that we can hear incorrectly and give voice to the spirit of deception if we are filtering things improperly. If we are tuned solely to worldly values, we will miss it. If we are filtering everything through our own ideas and biases, we will miss it. We can become captive of the very thing we want to avoid if the measuring stick we are using is skewed by a worldly system of assessment.

Good People Deceived

I have seen so many good people give place to the voice of deception because of their personal biases, leanings, and methods. That is not to say they were bad or evil people. I am not even saying that their biases or leanings were inherently evil. However, it attributed to their inability to hear the voice of the Lord clearly. Preconceptions can dull one's hearing and prevent them from exercising correct discernment.

Peter could not comprehend what Jesus said would take place. In the mind of Peter, it was of absolute certainty that Jesus was the Messiah that all Israel had awaited. He was confident that

Jesus would restore the nation and rid it of the evil Roman Empire. However, God's will and ways were different from what Peter imagined. Peter's predisposed conviction of how things were to transpire caused him to give voice to words of deception.

The image Peter possessed of Jesus was of a conquering king returning from battle. The picture Jesus painted was one of a suffering lamb sent to take away the sin of the world. Since these two pictures were irreconcilable in Peter's mind, he felt it was his duty to correct Jesus and put things aright. He sincerely believed he was saying and doing the right thing.

There is no doubt in my mind that Peter loved Jesus and was convinced that He was the way, truth, and life. Peter is the one who said, "You are the Christ, the Son of the living God" (Matthew 16:16). It was Peter to whom Jesus said, "Flesh and blood has not revealed this to you, but My Father in heaven" (Matthew 16:17). It was Peter who stayed with Jesus when others left him. Peter said there was no other place to go since Jesus was the only One who possessed the words of life.

How Can This Be?

So how does someone go from a position of being commended by Jesus to being rebuked and called satan? How can someone hear precisely from the Father at one moment and then later be out of tune with the heart of God? The answer is preconceptions, biases, and beliefs that are not based on the words of Jesus. Peter was thoroughly convinced that Jesus would not suffer at the hands of the Empire. He believed that Jesus would overcome the evil that was present and establish the kingdom of God on earth, beginning in Israel. However, Peter was wrong and therefore was deceived.

Once again, Peter's heart was not evil, but he had given place to the voice of deception through his beliefs and biases that were not in agreement with the words of Jesus. His misplaced convictions were elevated to the point that Jesus called him satan and told him that he was an offense.

We can love God and have His commendation; we may even prophesy and be accurate in our ministry. However, if we allow the things covered in this book to take hold of us, it will give way to the voice of deception within our lives. Good people can give place to a bad thing.

We must be able to separate that which is good from that which is God. It is possible for us to have a natural bias that is not evil; it may be good and wholesome. However, it can never be elevated to a place greater than what God has said and is presently saying. We cannot allow it to pollute our spiritual well to the point that the water we draw out becomes bitter. If we cannot subjugate our preconceptions and biases to the Word of God and the voice of the Holy Spirit, we will miss it and give place to the voice of deception.

> "Even my own familiar friend in whom I trusted,
> Who ate my bread, Has lifted up his
> heel against me" (Psalm 41:9).

The Psalmist expressly declared that a friend could do evil things. Most theologians ascribe this as a prophetic verse of Scripture that specifically pertained to Judas Iscariot betraying Jesus. However, I believe there is a principle that can be seen in this verse. A friend has the potential of being deceived and becoming a voice of deception.

Judas was one of the twelve disciples that Jesus initially chose to follow Him. He obviously exhibited some characteristics that qualified him to be part of the group because he became the treasurer and bookkeeper of Jesus' ministry. Typically, you have a trusted individual overseeing financial dealings, which is what Judas was responsible for managing. There is no indication that Judas mismanaged or misappropriated funds. For over three years, he faithfully executed his responsibility and did what Jesus asked. There was no apparent reason that Judas could not be trusted.

Ultimately, Judas betrayed Jesus. The man who was Jesus' trusted friend was deceived and then authored an act of deception. I am sure that Judas felt justified in some way for carrying out his treasonous act. I am sure his arguments and reasonings confirmed that he was doing the right thing. However, Judas was deceived and then committed the worst crime in the history of humanity; he betrayed the very Son of God. The voice of a trusted friend became the voice of betrayal and deception.

The Lie That Poses as Truth

The voice of deception is the lie that poses as the truth. It declares it is virtuous while it is only evil; it claims it is right when it is wrong. It will even say it is holy when it is completely unholy. It poses as good when it is clearly bad.

At the writing of this book, for the last two years, we have been amid the COVID-19 pandemic. I have been a Christian and in ministry for over 40 years, and I have never been more embarrassed about the behavior and conduct of some in the body of Christ. Some pastors and leaders have made statements concerning COVID, the vaccine, masks, and the 2020 election that have been far removed from the truth. There has been almost every type of conceivable behavior conducted by some pastors and leaders in the Church based on personal biases. Much of it has been appalling.

I have personally witnessed pastors boast about threatening store clerks for asking them to wear a mask. They bragged about it while believing it was a virtuous act. I have seen leaders in the Church post things on social media that were false and misleading, and this is just the tip of the iceberg. These ministers believed they were agents of illumination while they were doing these things.

I will not go into detail on all the things that I have personally witnessed because it is not my desire to condemn anyone. The fact that they believed their conduct was correct at the time is the larger problem. This reveals how the voice of deception will pose as the truth when it is only a lie.

It is never appropriate for any Christian to threaten someone with bodily harm for asking them to put on a face covering; this is not the spirit of Christ. If they do not agree, they can politely leave. Likewise, it is never virtuous to publish false and misleading information in the name of being an illuminator of truth. False statements and information will always be what the Bible calls lying. God hates the lying tongue.

A lie that poses as the truth is still a lie. Someone can believe it is true, but it will never make it the truth. The voice of deception is a grand make-up artist that can disguise itself. It requires spiritual discernment to recognize it.

"For false christs and false prophets will rise and show great
signs and wonders to deceive, if possible, even the elect"
(Matthew 24:24).

Jesus warned that there would be those who would be deceived
and come to deceive. He was referring to those who give place
to the voice of deception within their lives. The chilling part of
this verse is the last line; He said that it could possibly affect the
very elect. The word "elect" means *chosen or favorite*. Jesus was
referring to those who are saved.

We must understand that being saved does not, by itself,
prevent someone from being victimized by the voice of
deception. Someone can be filled with the Holy Spirit yet still
give place to the voice of deception.

This is the reality: Your favorite prophet can miss it and fall
prey to the voice of deception. Those who think that they
cannot err are the ones who will fall the quickest. Prophets who
believe it is impossible for them to miss it are the ones who
have already missed it; they are deceived. The truth is that
ANYONE can miss it if we do not guard ourselves. No one is
infallible. Anyone can allow a friend's voice to be the voice of
deception within their lives if they do not practice spiritual
discernment.

I do not share this to cause anyone to be afraid. However, we
should be circumspect and on guard. We must examine
ourselves and ensure that we are not being moved by our biases
and preconceptions in hearing the voice of the Lord. We must
keep our spiritual wells clean and pure through meditation on
the Word of God and praying in the Spirit.

One of the key components of overcoming deception is recognizing that it exists and that anyone can fall prey. Your spiritual strength may be that you can hear God speak clearly. However, an unguarded strength can become a double weakness in anyone's life.

Pray this with me:

Father, I ask in Jesus' name that you would make me keen in the spirit. Rid me of any misconception, bias, or leaning that would prevent me from hearing Your voice clearly. Deliver me of anything that may be polluting my spiritual well. I break the power of the voice of deception in Jesus' name! Amen.

VOICES 2

3

JUSTIFYING YOUR ACTIONS

> Then the serpent said to the woman, "You will
> not surely die. For God knows that in the day
> you eat of it your eyes will be opened, and you
> will be like God, knowing good and evil." So
> when the woman saw that the tree was good
> for food, that it was pleasant to the eyes, and a
> tree desirable to make one wise, she took of its
> fruit and ate. She also gave to her husband with
> her, and he ate (Genesis 3:4-6).

One of the tools the enemy uses to ensnare believers is the voice
of justification and rationalization. If you observe in this
passage of Scripture, there were justifications the serpent spoke
to Eve that capitalized on her own desires.

The enemy said three specific things that baited the hook of
deception, which helped Eve justify and rationalize her actions.
The first thing he said was, *"You will not die."* Secondly, he said,
"Your eyes will be opened." The third point he spoke was, *"You
will be like God."*

I Promise, This Won't Hurt

One of the first things the enemy speaks to someone to cause them to sin is, *"This will not hurt anyone; it's ok."* The voice of justification always seeks to ensure a person that negative consequences will not result from a sinful action. So, if no one will be hurt, why not do it? This logic is the language of the voice of justification and rationalization. It always seeks to convince its victims that everything will be alright and no one will be harmed. However, the moment someone takes the bait, its venom of deception will be released.

The voice of justification works like a doctor giving someone poison while telling them it is the cure for their disease. It promises life on the other side of an action that will only produce death and destruction. Once someone believes the voice of justification, they become convinced that they are right in doing something that is wrong. Some of the most heinous crimes throughout history were carried out by those who believed they were right in what they were doing.

Once Eve believed that her action would not harm her or anyone else, it was all downhill. She bought into the lie spoken by the voice of justification which started her down the rabbit hole of deception and destruction. One moment she was sitting pretty; the next moment found her naked and hiding from God. In the blink of an eye, Adam and Eve went from life to death, righteousness to sin, wealth to poverty, home to homeless, and clothed to naked. Their fall was all a result of rationalization and justification produced by the lies of satan.

Your Eyes Will Be Opened

The voice of justification did not end with the declaration that no harm would come to anyone. It proceeded to declare, *"Your eyes will be opened."* Who would not want to see more clearly? Certainly, this must be something that God desires one to possess. Clearer vision will undoubtedly help to fulfill the purpose of God. Can you see where this continues to lead?

The voice of justification opens the door for human rationalization; they work in tandem with each other. Unfortunately, many Christians consistently fall prey to this tactic of the enemy. They rationalize away the need for obedience so they can justify disobedience and rebellion. The voice of justification is always nearby to provide an excuse to refrain from obeying God and giving way to their flesh.

Man has always desired spiritual illumination. It is programmed within the DNA of humanity to pursue insight and understanding because God created us in that manner. There is a deep desire within all of us to receive spiritual illumination and insight concerning things that are concealed from us. The voice of justification convinced Eve that the way to attain this insight was to eat the forbidden fruit. If she just took the plunge, she would have access to all knowledge that was previously hidden.

The voice of justification delivered the exact opposite of what it promised Eve. It promised light but instead brought darkness. It promised illumination but only produced blindness. It promised wisdom from on high but only delivered ignorance through sin. Hear this: the devil is a liar, and there is no truth in him.

The enemy's voice will tell you that a wrong deed is the right thing to do. It attempts to give you license to do something that is sinful. I have repeatedly said that having a right to do something does not make it the right thing to do. There is an enormous difference between your rights and what is right. The voice of satan will always provide justification for wrong and sinful behavior in the name of "it is your right."

Your Right Doesn't Make It Right

Those of us who are American citizens are aware of our rights. These rights we possess are wonderful and should be cherished. However, there are times that believers confuse Americanism with Christianity. Believers with an extreme "rights" driven disposition can become non-Christlike while believing they are merely exercising their rights. The justification for their behavior becomes "it is my right, so it is right." However, your rights and what is right are two different things.

As an American, the rights you possess do not mean it is right for you to do something. For instance, up until the 2022 ruling of the Supreme Court that overturned Roe v Wade, every woman in the United States had a right to terminate their pregnancy with an abortion. However, their right does not make it the right thing to do. The constitutional right touted by many did not change the fact that it is wrong to kill an unborn child and stop a beating heart.

Every adult American has the right to drink alcohol and get drunk. It is a right we possess that people fought to secure. Many Americans drink alcohol regularly and get drunk on a semi-regular basis. Yet, drunkenness is still sinful. God's Word does not change based upon the rights that you may possess. The right we possess does not make it right.

In America, homosexuals now have a constitutional right to marry each other. State laws cannot forbid same-sex marriage. Once again, the right does not make it right. The Bible strictly forbids homosexual behavior; it is sinful. God does not recognize any homosexual marriage because the act violates Scripture. It is the wrong thing to do, even if it is one's right to do so.

Paul specifically commanded Christians never to use their liberties and rights to justify fleshly behavior. He went on to say that we are to serve one another through the love of God. Paraphrased, Paul said that if you have a right to do something, you should refrain from doing it if it hurts someone else. As believers, we must walk in God's love by doing no harm to our neighbors. Having a right to do something cannot become the justification for any believer doing anything that potentially harms someone else.

You Will Be like God

In the garden, the voice of justification continued by telling Eve that she would be like God. Think about that. Who doesn't want to be like God? Why reject such a wonderful offer? If we were like God, His job would be easier. We could take a load off His platter by being like Him. Can you see how the voice of justification, combined with human reasoning, sends someone down the road of destruction? This is what happened to Adam and Eve.

Justification seems to find its way to the root of all sinful behavior. Even blatant rebellion will defend itself with the voice of justification. We see this in the life of King Saul:

Then Samuel went to Saul, and Saul said to him, "Blessed are you of the LORD! I have performed the commandment of the LORD." But Samuel said, "What then is this bleating of the sheep in my ears, and the lowing of the oxen which I hear?" And Saul said, "They have brought them from the Amalekites; for the people spared the best of the sheep and the oxen, to sacrifice to the LORD your God; and the rest we have utterly destroyed." Then Samuel said to Saul, "Be quiet! And I will tell you what the LORD said to me last night." And he said to him, "Speak on." So Samuel said, "When you were little in your own eyes, were you not head of the tribes of Israel? And did not the LORD anoint you king over Israel? Now the LORD sent you on a mission, and said, 'Go, and utterly destroy the sinners, the Amalekites, and fight against them until they are consumed.' Why then did you not obey the voice of the LORD? Why did you swoop down on the spoil, and do evil in the sight of the LORD?" And Saul said to Samuel, "But I have obeyed the voice of the LORD, and gone on the mission on which the LORD sent me, and brought back Agag king of Amalek; I have utterly destroyed the Amalekites. But the people took of the plunder, sheep and oxen, the best of the things which should have been utterly destroyed, to sacrifice to the LORD your God in Gilgal." So Samuel said: "Has the LORD as great delight in burnt offerings and sacrifices, As in obeying the voice of the

LORD? Behold, to obey is better than sacrifice, And to heed than the fat of rams. For rebellion is as the sin of witchcraft, And stubbornness is as iniquity and idolatry. Because you have rejected the word of the LORD, He also has rejected you from being king" (1 Samuel 15:13-23).

This Bible passage tells a tragic story. God commanded Saul to destroy the Amalekites totally; he was to leave nothing alive. However, Saul spared the king and brought back the best oxen and sheep, which he said would be used as a sacrifice to the Lord.

Once he was confronted by the prophet Samuel, he did three things. He lied, denied, and justified. First, he **lied** by saying he had performed what he was commanded to do. Then when Samuel explained the things he failed to do, Saul **denied** that he failed to obey and doubled down on his story. He then **justified** his actions by saying that it was for a good reason: to offer up sacrifices.

I believe when King Saul first went on his mission, he fully intended to do exactly what Samuel instructed him to do. However, once things began to transpire, the voice of justification and rationalization began to speak through the people near him.

Instead of saying, "*I have specific instructions from the Lord that I am responsible for carrying out,*" he said, "*What Liah-maniah said makes sense, so guys, there's a change in plans.*" The voice of justification gave him an escape from obeying God's command. However, Samuel said these actions were rebellion on the part of Saul.

Common Sense and Revenge

The voice of justification can seem harmless when it masks itself in supposed common sense or a better idea. It hides its motive by appealing to human reasoning and often functions in tandem with it. However, its end objective is always the same; it seeks to steal, kill, and destroy.

Unfortunately, many believers yield to the voice of justification. They fall prey to its bidding because they fail to discern properly. They believe it is common sense speaking when it is actually the voice of the enemy, the voice of justification.

At the root of vengeful behavior is this dangerous voice that says, *"They did this to me, so I have the right to do it back to them."* It will even twist Scripture verses, such as "An eye for an eye, and a tooth for a tooth." It will use these things to manipulate believers into sinful behaviors that are antithetical to Christian conduct. Jesus said to turn the other cheek. He said to go the extra mile and be merciful to others. He said to do good to those who despitefully use you. Yes, that is what Jesus said!

If you believe it is right for you to retaliate against someone because of a wrong done, you are listening to the voice of justification. This voice has caused people to do evil things. It has caused people to be malicious to others in the name of evening the score. It has provoked some to murder people they believed had wronged them. The great tragedy is that those who do such things believe they are right in doing so. Any voice that legitimizes hatred, retaliation, or revenge is not the voice of the Lord; it is the voice of the devil.

Justification or Repentance

One of the most dangerous aspects of the voice of justification is that it prevents the act of repentance. When people believe they are right in doing something wrong, they will not repent. They will not change their course of behavior. Instead, they will continue to sin and do it passionately.

It is bad when people sin and realize they are sinning. However, it is much worse when people sin yet believe they are righteous in the sin they are committing. In these situations, there is little hope for true heart repentance.

I believe that if King Saul had immediately responded to the confrontation of Samuel with brokenness and repentance, God would have allowed him to remain king. Saul's biggest sin was that he listened to the voice of justification and allowed it to take control of his life. God is near to those with a contrite spirit but far from those who justify themselves.

When you consider the life of King David, he performed a great atrocity by committing adultery with a woman and having her husband killed. By my measuring stick, that is worse than sparing the life of a king and bringing back some beasts of the field. The significant difference between Saul and David is that when confronted by the voice of the Lord, one justified their behavior while the other repented of their sin. Saul was controlled by the voice of justification, while David heeded the voice of conviction.

We must identify this voice of justification as our enemy's voice. It must be revealed for what it is. Any voice that excuses you from the responsibility of doing what is right or gives you justification for wrong behavior is the voice of the devil. Although we should abstain from all manner of sin, the greater sin is to continue being led by the voice of justification. It will cause the forfeiting of purpose and destiny as it did in the life of Saul.

Blame Shifting

We observe that after Adam and Eve sinned, they realized they were naked. As a result, they made coverings out of fig leaves and hid from the Lord. When God came to fellowship and commune with them in the cool of the evening, He had to call out to Adam to locate him and get him out of hiding.

As Adam began to dialogue with the Lord, he was posed a question. God asked, *"Did you eat from the tree?"* Instead of Adam saying, *"Yes, I did, and I am sorry, please forgive me,"* he said, *"Lord, the WOMAN that YOU gave to me, SHE gave it to me!"* Adam successfully blamed the only two intelligent beings he knew on the entire planet in one breath. He blamed God and Eve simultaneously; he accepted no responsibility.

Likewise, when God asked Eve about the situation, she said, *"The serpent told me to do it."* It was like a moment from classic television between Flip Wilson and Geraldine. Eve said, *"The devil made me do it!"* She successfully blamed the serpent and denied any responsibility.

Here is what can be derived from this account: When someone heeds the voice of justification, they blame others for their actions and refrain from accepting responsibility.

Mercy Forfeited

Please hear this: Failure to accept responsibility for your wrong or sinful actions prevents mercy from being extended. Blaming others for your sin causes the forfeiture of mercy in your own life. God will extend mercy and grace to those who are broken and contrite, who admit to their mistakes and take responsibility. This is what Adam and Eve needed to do the most but failed to do at all.

It is likely that their outcome could have been different if they had removed themselves from the path of justification. Sincere repentance could have changed Adam and Eve's trajectory. Instead, they doubled down on their mistake and justified their actions. This response caused them to lose everything.

Throughout my years of ministry, I have seen this pattern repeat itself in the lives of believers. They blame others for their actions as they rehearse the voices that bring justification for sinful behavior. Many times, the voices they are listening to are well-meaning friends that only aid in digging a deeper hole for them to dwell. Sometimes it may be a family member who genuinely cares for them but fails to realize they are enabling poor decisions. Unfortunately, this is an all-too-common problem.

There is always a voice somewhere that will say what you want to hear. Likewise, there is always a voice somewhere that will justify the vilest behavior, regardless of what it may be.

A National Disgrace

On January 6, 2021, we witnessed an awful event broadcast on every news outlet. A riot took place at the United States

Capitol involving thousands of people who were unhappy about the election results. The people who gathered believed that election fraud was responsible for President Donald Trump losing the 2020 Presidential Election. They also believed that the official certification of the results had to be stopped.

During the official ballot casting in the Senate, a mass of people unlawfully broke into the halls of Congress. They ransacked both the inside and outside. Congressmen's offices were invaded, property was destroyed, and the place where our nation's law are made was desecrated. Gallows were built outside the Capitol building as people called for the lynching of the Vice-President and other elected officials.

This invasion resulted in five people losing their lives, and over 140 police officers being injured. Some of these officers who had previously served in the military said it was worse than anything they had ever experienced on the field of combat.

I am not attempting to comment on the accuracy of the election results. I am not commenting on the appropriateness of their protest. Neither am I offering a commentary on what many of the rally speakers said preceding this uprising.

Whether you agree with the cause of these rioters or not, and regardless of who was actively responsible, this was a national disgrace. It defied all manner of law and order. Jesus was nowhere present in any of the rioter's lawlessness. At the root of all this was the voice of justification. It led a group of American citizens, many who were Christians, down a road of violence and attempted insurrection.

Shocked!

After all the dust settled, I was surprised at how many Christian leaders and believers justified the actions of those who unlawfully invaded the Capitol. I heard some say this needed to happen. Some said that whatever had to be done to overturn the election results should be carried out.

To say that I was surprised and shocked is an understatement. It was challenging for me to comprehend how Christians, along with some Church leaders, could condone lawless behavior that intended to harm the innocent, which resulted in injuries to law enforcement officials. Much to my disappointment, there were some Spirit-filled Christians who praised the actions of those who violated the law and acted inappropriately. I am confident that if the tables were turned and the other political side had done these things, these perpetrators would have said it was demonic.

This event is a prime example of how the voice of justification can invade the life of a believer. This is how it works within the mind and heart of an individual: *"I disagree with what is happening, and something needs to change. I am an agent of change. I will do something about it to ensure no one else encounters this same injustice. Therefore, any means necessary to secure my desire is the right thing to do, even if it requires lawlessness or rebellion. The end justifies the means."* This thinking is the rehearsed narrative of a person duped by this misleading voice.

The voices of fleshly justification and rationalization are demonic. They work in conjunction with the voice of deception. They interact with one another to hatch a plan of sin and destruction, and we witnessed this on January 6, 2021.

There was a group of people, many of them Christians, who gave their ear to the voice of justification. It caused good people to make poor decisions and do bad things. The voice of justification caused unlawful actions to become virtuous in the minds of those who yielded to it.

Not The First Time

There is no doubt that many military dictators who committed genocide believed they were on a holy mission. They thought that they were justified in the wholesale slaughter of innocent lives. They gave their ear over to the voice of justification, giving them rational reasons for committing their atrocity, and the enemy's plan was conceived and brought forth. These things have been repeated historically numerous times.

Even today, a military conflict began at the time of this writing between Ukraine and Russia. The leader of Russia, Vladimir Putin, gave numerous fallacious justifications for his unprovoked invasion of Ukraine. In the meantime, Ukrainian civilians and soldiers have lost their lives due to these attacks. The entire world condemned his actions, yet he believes his mission is virtuous. Killing innocent citizens is legitimized and rationalized in the mind of a man deceived by the voice of justification.

Guard Yourself

While most believers will never have the power to wage war like many ungodly dictators, the same voices that control them can affect Christians in various areas of their lives. When someone gives ear to the voice of justification, evil becomes virtuous in their own mind. This is a deceptive voice that can destroy believers' lives. It must be identified, called out, and eradicated within the body of Christ.

We must be on guard against this voice that seeks to destroy the lives of believers. I want to repeat something I said earlier: **There is always a voice somewhere that will justify wrong and sinful behavior.** Many times, it can be the voice of a friend, coworker, fellow church member, politician, or even a pastor. However, sinful behavior can never be justified. We must crush this evil voice with the light of God's Word and the illumination of His Spirit.

Pray this with me today:

Father, I receive your forgiveness for any area where I have listened to or heeded the voice of justification. Give me eyes to see and ears to hear so that I can identify this wicked voice at work. I thank You today for empowering me to do what is right in Your sight and not my own. In Jesus' name, I ask these things. Amen.

VOICES 2

4

OFFENSE & BITTERNESS

Follow peace with all men, and holiness, without which no man shall see the Lord: Looking diligently lest any man fail of the grace of God; lest any root of bitterness springing up trouble you, and thereby many be defiled; (Hebrews 12:14-15, KJV).

It would be impossible to discuss all the different voices in the world today. However, I will discuss in this writing some of the more common voices that regularly victimize undiscerning Christians. I have witnessed the actions of these voices throughout my experience in ministry and as a pastor. The voice of offense is one such voice that can produce devastating effects on family and church relationships.

A Personal Experience

In 1987, I was employed by a leading national ministry as their worship leader. About a year later, some things happened that caused me to become offended. In December of 1988, after serving there for about one year, I recall waking up one morning around 2 am. I began to pray as I sensed the Lord was speaking to me.

As I prayed, I kept sensing God was speaking for me to leave my employment and that He had greater things in store for me. I was convinced that the Lord was saying it was my time to exit. After all, it had to be the Lord speaking since I woke up at 2 am for Him to talk to me, right?

Soon after this, I shared the story with a fellow minister. I also told them some of my complaints. These were the things that had produced the offense in my life. They, in turn, shared our conversation with the Senior Apostle of the ministry, Dr. Bill Hamon. After he heard the story, I received a call from him requesting a meeting. My wife and I hurried back to meet with him.

During the meeting, he confronted me about the things I had said. I admitted to him that I articulated many of the items in question. He then looked at me and said, "God is not telling you to leave; He is actually wanting you to make a five-year commitment!" Wow! I was floored! This was diametrically opposed to everything that I believed I heard from the Lord. Bishop Hamon then asked me to give a five-year commitment right there at that moment. I said, "Yes, I commit to five years and as long as the Lord desires me to be here."

Immediately following that confrontation, we started experiencing miraculous interventions in various areas of our lives. Ministry opportunities suddenly evolved, and financial breakthroughs materialized. Within six months, we were able to purchase our first home. Things began to fall into place. Hallelujah!

The reason I share this story is to point this out to you: The voice I thought belonged to the Lord was, in reality, the voice of offense. My offense was speaking to me as it disguised itself in deception. Its goal was to separate me from the place where God had planted me and from the people to which He had joined me. This voice desired to short-circuit my divine destiny and thwart breakthroughs in my life. **I believe that if I had heeded the voice of offense, I would have forfeited the blessing. Think about it!**

The Root of Offense

Offense has a voice that is usually rooted in the mind and emotions. It is often instigated and aroused through hurt or disagreement caused by another individual or group of people. It can result from something said or done that angers or brings emotional pain to the offended party. When this happens, the voice of offense will begin speaking. The greater the offense, the louder the voice will seem.

It is important to recognize that living in a fallen world will inevitably cause things to be said and done with the potential of producing offense. Every person alive today has probably been offended by the actions of someone or did something to offend another, whether intentional or not. We have all experienced these things before.

The goal of the voice of offense is to produce hurt, bitterness, separation, slander, hatred, and other works of the flesh. It seeks to drive wedges between God-ordained relationships and causes believers to become bitter toward one another. The purpose is to discourage, destroy, and dismantle the things that God desires so the kingdom of darkness can have free reign within the lives of its victims.

Listening to the voices of offense can cause believers to engage in wicked behavior. Once someone surrenders to this voice, true and accurate spiritual discernment ceases. It often results in gossip, slander, false accusations, and bitterness, to name a few. These behaviors are clearly defined as sin throughout the Bible. As a rule, anytime you speak negatively about an individual to anyone other than someone who can do something about the situation, you are engaging in gossip and slander.

Manipulation and Witchcraft

When someone slanders an individual and makes false accusations against them, they are operating in ungodly control and manipulation. It is not merely a "venting" of emotions. Attempting to maliciously provoke negative opinions of anyone in the mind of others is the sin of witchcraft. When the motive is to defame and destroy, this is particularly true. Doing this in the name of "the Lord told me" makes it worse, bordering on blasphemy. This type of spiritual justification of ungodly behavior is the very height of deception.

The Holy Spirit will never tell anyone to engage in slanderous and divisive behavior. We should never tear down or destroy others within the body of Christ. Our ministry is quite the contrary; it is to edify, encourage, and build up one another.

Once someone begins to give themself over to the voice of offense, it will lead them down a path of deceit and deception. Things will be exaggerated and fabricated in their minds. Distortions of the truth will become more real than facts. Their reality becomes an ever-increasing lie that will not resemble the truth in any manner.

When things are born out of the voice of offense, the wicked fruit of bitterness and rebellion will ensue. The actions that result from listening to these false voices can conjure demonic activity. Wicked fabrications of the mind, along with demonic alternate realities, begin to surface. This will, in turn, result in the sin of witchcraft. Samuel identified this evolution when he told King Saul that rebellion is as the sin of witchcraft.

The Path of Deceit and Deception

I have seen people offended about something that happened to them. Instead of forgiving the individual they believe wronged them, they heeded the voice of offense, and it took them down the road of exaggeration. The perceived pain of the offense was transformed into something totally removed from reality as the enemy's lies took root. The voice of offense created and spoke false narratives diametrically opposed to the actual truth. Their hearts conceived vain imaginations as they listened to this heinous voice.

From there, they proceeded to slander the individual whom they believed wronged them. The stories and narratives that gushed from them continued growing to the point that the truth in their mind became a lie. The only thing these people could see was the false image that the devil painted on the canvas of their hearts.

The awful thing about the voice of offense is that it is heard by the offended person and then echoed to others. The offense they took is then projected and proclaimed to their friends and acquaintances, hoping that others will take the same affront. The voice of offense affects many people through just one event, and it multiplies and reproduces itself through talebearing and gossip. This voice is evil to its core. Its goal is to destroy and dismantle God-ordained relationships.

Offense Is a Liar

I have witnessed people offended over things that did not actually happen. However, they believed in their own mind that something hurtful was inflicted in their life by another individual. Regardless of the facts, they continued to listen to the voice of offense. They lived in an alternate reality created by the lies of a demonic spirit. The movie broadcast in their mind was nothing more than a fabricated fantasy from the studio of hell.

Then they decided to share their offense with everyone. The venom of their perceived hurt was spewed through the false voice they continued to heed. Their goals were to slander, accuse, and defame. However, they justified their poisonous rhetoric by telling people they were merely warning others and being agents of enlightenment. Lies were continually fabricated and replicated as their false scenario continued with a new episode daily.

We must understand that the voice of offense is a liar. It will not only speak untruthful things but will also give false justifications for its actions. This voice is wicked and full of dangerous intent.

Abominable Behavior

These types of behaviors are abominable to God and harmful to the body of Christ. The person harmed the most is the one who yields to the voice of offense by allowing their mouth to be the gate of expression. The seeds sowed with the words of their mouth not only hurts others who listen, but it also produces a harvest of pain and suffering for them. We must avoid these things by walking in love, grace, and forgiveness.

There are proper ways to share a grievance. However, slander, gossip, and railing accusations are never appropriate actions for believers. These are fleshly and devilish ways that people attempt to resolve a spiritual issue. Malicious defamation of someone with untruthful statements is demonic behavior. We must avoid these things like a deadly plague and choose to walk in love. After all, this is what Jesus commanded us to do.

Absalom's Offense

When you read the account of Absalom, you will see the event which caused him to spiral down a rabbit hole. His sister, Tamar, was raped by his half-brother, Amnon (2 Samuel 13). Tamar told Absalom what happened; he, in turn, told his sister to keep it to herself and not take it to heart. However, Absalom allowed the voice of offense to direct his life from that time forward. Everything we read that took place in Absalom's life was dictated by the voice of offense. He became a marionette on strings controlled by a puppet master named Offense and Bitterness.

We read what happened in Absalom's life:

"And Absalom spoke to his brother Amnon neither good nor bad. For Absalom hated Amnon, because he had forced his sister Tamar" (2 Samuel 13:22).

Absalom told his sister not to take to heart what happened to her (don't be offended). However, he listened to the voice of offense, walked in unforgiveness, and became bitter. He should have listened to his own advice. Absalom's acts of taking offense and walking in unforgiveness were the things that sent him down the road of destruction.

Jesus said if your brother offends you, go to him. He also said to love your enemy, but Absalom refused to speak to his brother and hated him. As a result, Absalom cultivated a root of bitterness within his heart. By refusing to talk to Amnon, he fertilized the seeds of offense. Absalom's hatred grew as he listened to the voice of offense and walked in unforgiveness. Ultimately, the root of bitterness was planted so deep within his life that he murdered Amnon two years later.

Time Makes It Worse

There was a two-year time lapse between the time when Tamar was raped and the murder of Amnon. However, Absalom began to plot his revenge on the day his sister was raped.

"... for only Amnon is dead. For by the command of Absalom this has been determined from the day that he forced his sister Tamar" (2 Samuel 13:32).

Absalom had already planned and plotted the murder of Amnon from day one. The voice of offense spoke to him daily and gave him justification to murder his brother. For two years, he planned and meditated on it. For two years, he fantasized about Amnon's blood being spilled. Then, finally, at the right moment, his plan was hatched.

For two years, Absalom could have been working on removing the offense. For two years, he could have been declaring forgiveness and dialoguing with his brother. Instead, he chose to embrace the vicious cycle of offense, unforgiveness, and bitterness. He opened the door for the enemy, and the devil obliged him.

Double the Sinner

Absalom's story is tragic. He was David's son, a prince in the kingdom in line for the throne. However, he forfeited his purpose and destiny because he listened to the wrong voice. Absalom gave his ear over to the voice of offense which produced bitterness and hatred. This action culminated in the murder of his own brother.

Everything that God destined him to become in the kingdom of Israel was flushed down the toilet. He did not lose everything because of something done to him personally, but because he listened to the voice of offense. While Absalom's anger was understandable, it did not make his actions right. Someone may have a natural justification for being angry, but it never justifies unforgiveness and bitterness. That is the road to disaster.

Later in Absalom's life, he became twice the sinner. Although his half-brother raped his sister, Absalom committed sexual sin with all of his father's concubines in plain view of the nation.

"So they pitched a tent for Absalom on the top of the house, and Absalom went in to his father's concubines in the sight of all Israel" (2 Samuel 16:22).

The very thing that Absalom abhorred Amnon for doing, he did to a greater degree in front of the nation. Absalom was empowered and justified by the voice of offense to which he was heeding. **The voice that promised him revenge is the voice that robbed him of his destiny.** The voice that promised to even the score caused him to be the joker who became the tragedy of Israel.

Forgive and Refrain

In John 20:23, Jesus said whoever's sins you retain, they are retained and whoever's sins you forgive, they are forgiven. Jesus was not giving His disciples power to forgive people of their sins. Rather, He was articulating a spiritual principle showing that sin is released from you when you choose to forgive. Forgiveness will shut the mouth of the voice of offense and keep you from repeating the same action. The act of forgiveness disables sin from reproducing both in and through you.

However, when you choose to walk in unforgiveness, you retain that sin and give place to the voice of offense. This voice will become increasingly louder to the point that you will be deafened to the voice of the Holy Spirit. The sin you retain is the open door for the enemy to build a stronghold within your life. This is what happened to Absalom.

Ultimately, Absalom was destroyed, and his father wept at the news of his death. Absalom's demise was self-inflicted; he brought it upon himself through an open door to the voice of offense. Many believe Absalom's downfall came because he led a rebellion. However, the uprising was merely a manifestation of the root of bitterness caused by the voice of offense screaming in his ear. His sin did not begin as a rebellion; it started by listening to the wrong voice. **The root of rebellion against his own father, David, was rooted in giving place to the voice of offense. Think about it!**

The Evil Voice Is at the Root

At the root of what many have referred to as the Absalom spirit is the voice of offense. Typically, those who operate with this spirit are not motivated to lead a rebellion in the beginning stages. Instead, they open the door to rebellion by listening to fleshly and demonic voices. This voice justifies their hearts and minds for divisive and rebellious behavior.

As a rule, the fruit manifested through sinful behavior is not the root. The fruit of rebellion typically has a root starting with an emotional wound that opens the door for corresponding voices to take advantage of the situation. Listening to these voices and doing their bidding is at the root, even more so than the wound or hurt that opened the door. The wound may have been the seed, but by listening to the voice of offense, it turned into a root of bitterness.

In the case of Absalom, he was emotionally hurt that his sister was raped by his brother. As a result, he began listening to the voice of offense which led to bitterness, hatred, and the need for vengeance. This sin gave way to fleshly justifications in his mind that murder was acceptable.

I am sure his argument was, *"Since no one else is going to do anything about this, I will."* His father, David, was displeased with what happened to Tamar; however, he never took any corrective action. Most likely, Absalom was upset with his father for doing nothing, and it opened the doorway for the voice of offense and justification. It was truly a witches' brew, a horrible combination of things that led him down the path of destruction.

Change the Voice to Change Behavior

Many times, when we see people conducting their lives in an improper manner, we evaluate things by what we see on the surface. Doing this leads us to attempt behavioral modification in the lives of those who are misbehaving. However, I have found that at the root of all sinful behavior is an ungodly voice that one is heeding. When people listen to the wrong voice, they will behave wrong. When they listen to the right voice, they will behave right.

If a person alters their behavior while continuing to listen to the same wrong voices, the change will be short-lived. Until someone changes the voices to which they are listening, their behavior and conduct will not permanently be transformed.

> Pursue peace with all people, and holiness, without which no one will see the Lord: looking carefully lest anyone fall short of the grace of God; lest any root of bitterness springing up cause trouble, and by this many become defiled (Hebrews 12:14-15).

Let's look at this passage of Scripture again. Bitterness results from repeatedly listening to the voice of offense and refusing to forgive someone. The echoes of the event that brought the initial hurt repeat themselves like an endless chorus of pain and suffering. The more it is heard, the stronger the root of bitterness becomes within an individual.

It is interesting that the writer of Hebrews uses the terminology "root of bitterness." We can see from this verse of Scripture that bitterness is a root. While bitterness is the result of listening to the voice of offense, it becomes a root in someone's life that will produce a tremendous amount of undesirable fruit. It will grow into the fruit of malice, hatred, envy, murder, slander, gossip, and rage, to name a few. These are things that Christians are commanded to refrain from doing.

Sometimes we may say a particular person has an issue with gossip, slander, or back-biting. However, the problem with their mouth is only the fruit of something worse inside them. The root within their heart is bitterness produced by the continual operation of the voice of offense. Therefore, the real culprit of the situation is not the lack of discipline for their tongue; it is the root that developed within their heart due to listening to the wrong voice.

Bitterness Forfeits God's Grace

The word "grace" in Hebrews 12:15 (the writer speaking of falling short of the grace of God) is defined by **Strong's Dictionary** as divine influence upon the heart. This verse declares that the root of bitterness is an indication that one is falling short of God's influence upon their life. Therefore, allowing bitterness to take root in one's life will cause them to forfeit divine influence. In other words, they will cease to hear the voice of the Lord clearly. God's voice will no longer influence them as bitterness takes root.

When Christians listen to the voice of offense and allow bitterness to form a stronghold, this cycle will happen repeatedly. They forfeit the ability to hear the voice of the Lord clearly, mistaking illegitimate voices for God's voice. They listen to things that tell them to separate from God-ordained relationships. The voices of justification shout in their ears and give them reasons for their unbiblical behavior. This behavior is what the root of bitterness produces.

Walking in Love

Walking in love is the cure for offense and bitterness. It will stop the voice of offense and the root of bitterness. Walking in love silences the voice of offense. The love of God enables us to tune out the voices of hurt, which ultimately leads people down the path of deception. Walking in love keeps our hearts pure and our spirits tuned to the voice of the Lord, our Shepherd. It prevents us from following the voice of a stranger.

The voice of the Lord will always be the voice of love since He is love. His voice is filled with His love for you and me. If it is not love, it is not God. If it is hatred, it proceeds from satan. If it is bitter, it comes from the pit of hell. Love is the language of God and why the apostle Paul said that love is the fulfillment of all the law. When we walk in the love of God, we will walk in obedience and not harm our neighbor.

Love is the frequency upon which heaven's communications are broadcast. If we fail to tune to heaven's frequency, we will miss heaven's broadcast. Therefore, it is imperative that we walk in love for us to hear the voice of the Lord correctly. Love is needed to properly discern the voices that we hear.

Pray this with me today:

Father, I ask you to forgive me for allowing the voice of offense to operate within my life. I choose to forgive anyone who has wronged me. Empower me to walk in Your love toward everyone around me. I renounce offense, the root of bitterness, and all its fruit in the name of Jesus. Amen.

VOICES 2

5

What I Want to Hear

> For the time will come when they will not take
> the true teaching; but, **moved by their desires**,
> they will get for themselves a great number of
> teachers for the pleasure of hearing them; And
> shutting their ears to what is true, will be
> turned away to belief in foolish stories (2
> Timothy 4:3-4, BBE).

There are many people today who say they are looking for the truth. They declare they want to know the truth concerning the many ongoing situations in the world. Some say they desire truth; however, more often than not, they are merely looking for someone to say what they want to hear. These people are looking for a voice that will agree with the predisposition they have taken. They want someone to say what they want to hear—someone to agree with their thoughts and beliefs.

Paul talked about people finding for themselves those who speak what they want to hear based upon their own bias. He said that many would go after foolish stories. Here is the truth: **There is always a voice somewhere that will agree with you and say what you want to hear.** There is usually more than just one of these voices in our internet world where anyone can possess a platform to say whatever they desire, regardless of what it may be and whether it is true or not.

At this writing, we are on the tail end of a worldwide coronavirus pandemic. Every imaginable story has been promoted and propagated concerning COVID over the last several years. People became impassioned in what they believed and were convinced that they were the holders of the truth. In their minds, they became the protectors of the Holy Grail. After all, they read an article on social media by an unknown expert sent to them by their friend, so it must be true (sarcasm intended).

It is incredible how much weight someone will give an article written by an unknown individual when it says what they want to hear. On the other hand, an article or interview from a reliable and respected individual will be discounted and discarded when it fails to articulate the reader's bias. One of the most significant determining factors of the voices that someone will heed is that it says what they want to hear, and it aligns with their predisposition. If the voice contradicts their conviction, it will usually be ignored.

Mindsets Blind People to Truth

Mindsets are a leading reason that many people have difficulty discerning properly. It contributes to the inability of hearing and receiving truth. I have witnessed people with strong mindsets claim factual evidence was a lie, and the truth was found in disprovable statements. I have heard them say that their minds could not be changed regardless of contradictory evidence to what they believed. This problem became increasingly apparent as the world traversed many challenging issues. It has always been present; however, it has become magnified to a greater degree in recent days.

These things are merely symptomatic of an issue that must be overcome for Christians to properly discern the voices they hear. When someone is biased toward what they desire and are willing to listen, their hearing will be skewed. It is next to impossible to hear the right voice when a predilection has control of someone's mind.

The apostle Paul said people would refuse the truth because of their own desires. When people hear voices that articulate a desirable narrative, it is pleasurable to them. Conversely, when people hear voices that speak an undesirable message, it is confrontational to their thinking. Typically, they do not appreciate voices that are contradictory to their predisposed opinion and, therefore, will discard them. Sometimes they will even speak negatively about the opposing voices that challenge them.

I am sharing this so you can see the effects of wanting to hear something specific. When individual mindsets become entrenched in something that is not true, they will abhor the truth. When they become convinced that their opinion is infallible, they will shudder at any opposing thought or concept. Their perceived truth becomes nothing more than a myth based on the biases of their minds.

I have heard people say to me personally when they were told the truth concerning a situation, "*Please, don't tell me that; I don't want to hear it.*" They had been duped for so long and were genuinely convinced of the accuracy of their beliefs that when the truth came out, they refused to hear it. Their lives were so intertwined with the lie that denying it would crush the house of cards that existed within their minds. The alternate reality they were living in would cease to exist with the admission of the truth. The only truth they wanted to hear was their predisposition echoed.

You Can Be Wrong

One of the keys to properly hearing and discerning voices is realizing that your present opinion can be wrong. If we are convinced that there is no possibility for any error or mistake, we seal our spiritual ears to hear only that with which we agree. It becomes impossible to hear anything else because our ears become closed to it.

There are some things we know that are unchangeable. The truth that Jesus is the only way to be saved is not up for debate. The fact that He is the only mediator between God and man can never be changed. Yes, my ears are closed to anything speaking contrary to these truths because it is the very foundation of the gospel. It is the cornerstone of our faith in Jesus Christ and His Word.

However, regarding things that are not explicitly stated in the Bible, decisions we make, and the discernment of things in the world, we must understand that our opinions and leanings can be incorrect. We must be open to pivoting our position when confronted by truth rather than discounting it because it is not what we want to hear. I am not speaking of living with an open mind as the world defines it. However, I am articulating an understanding we must possess so that we are not caught in the trap of only hearing what we desire based on our predisposed opinions.

Voices That Agree but Lie

There is always a voice that will speak what one wants to hear. If there is an issue in society, there is always a voice that will agree with your leaning. Let me give you some examples of how these voices operate and function.

During the Obama presidency, numerous stories and theories were floated. These notions were proclaimed on social media platforms and chat pages. Unfortunately, many Christians latched on to these stories simply because they did not like the President, and it justified their vitriol.

Toward the end of his last term, the theory was promoted that Obama was releasing the National Guard, would declare martial law, and then serve a third term. As you know, it NEVER happened. However, many believers promoted this story as gospel truth. This was just one of the many false theories promoted that capitalized on the fears of many. President Obama held many political positions with which I vehemently disagree (as with many other politicians). However, the dislike of a person's political position never justifies the propagation of something false in response.

Making untruthful statements against anyone is what the Bible calls gossip, slander, and bearing false witness. It is sinful and unholy behavior that is just as bad as stealing and adultery. Also included are false prognostications that Christians pretend never took place after it proves to be wrong. It is swept under the rug because many do not want to acknowledge the truth.

These kinds of things ruin our witness and make the Church look foolish. Believers must stop conducting their lives in this manner.

For some reason, many justify spreading rumors in the name of wanting people to be informed and enlightened. The deception of this line of thinking causes Christians to believe they are agents of the light even if they are promoting unproven theories. If confronted in any way, they become angry and indignant that someone challenged their new revelation. After all, they saw it on social media, so it is undeniable truth (sarcasm intended). In reality, this narrative agrees with what they believe and desire to be true about someone or something.

The "truth" is that decades ago, many false stories were quieted before they could make it to the ears and eyes of the public. However, with the advent of social media, any story can find traction with the right promotion. Unfortunately, if the narrative being promoted is something that people want to believe, it immediately becomes truth in their minds.

Infallible Proof and Evidence

Everything we believe as Christians concerning Jesus is based on facts. We do not believe in a fairy tale from Never Land that someone created in their own mind. The gospel of Jesus Christ and His Kingdom are based upon historical evidence along with infallible proof. Many of these proofs are stated in the Bible and are recorded in books penned by ancient historians.

Luke, the writer of the book of Acts, said that Jesus presented himself alive after His suffering with "many infallible proofs being seen" (Acts 1:3). He indicated that there was irrefutable evidence of Jesus' resurrection. Jesus was seen by all the apostles and many others on numerous occasions. His victory over death is not a fairy tale.

Everything we believe is based on factual evidence. It is a fact that Jesus lived and walked upon this earth. It is a fact that He performed signs, wonders, and miracles. It is a fact that He died and then rose again on the third day. These facts are the basis of our faith. They are all confirmed by numerous witnesses who have written their testimony.

It is important for us to realize that nothing is true solely because we believe or desire for it to be true. I can believe that the sky is green, but it does not make it true. A Muslim that believes the way to salvation is through Islam does not make it so. Believing that something occurred when there is no credible factual evidence to confirm it does not make it true.

When Facts No Longer Matter

We live in a day when it seems that facts no longer matter. The only evidence that many people need is a published internet story that confirms what they desire to hear and believe. Unfortunately, it may be filled with fallacious information void of facts, and many will still think it is true. If it is something they want to believe, then it is gospel truth. If it is a smear about an individual they do not like, then it is the truth.

This gullibility has given way for varied theories and rumors to have traction in the public square. Gullible individuals latch on to these theories even with no credible evidence. These, in turn, form opinions in people's minds that cause incorrect perspectives within their lives. They believe things to be true that never happened and will not happen in the future.

The moment people begin to walk down this path, it opens the door for increasing deception. Skewed human rationalization takes control as each false theory builds on the other. Before long, people live in an alternate reality void of facts and evidence. It is a world they created in their own minds that is devoid of truth because facts have been discounted and dismissed. It is their own Neverland. To disbelieve one element of their perceived truth could potentially cause their entire manufactured world to collapse. Therefore, they cling to their theories as a parched man clings to a cup of water.

There are so many sensational, tantalizing stories floating around right now. People give voice to them regularly, but we all need to be careful not to fall for everything being proclaimed. **In particular, we should never put "thus says the Lord" at the end of a theory!**

Tabloid Christianity

I remember going to the grocery store with my parents when I was a child. Every checkout stand had an assortment of magazines and newspapers, and most of which were considered tabloid journalism publications. Even as a young boy, I was taught that these papers and magazines published questionable sensational stories. I recognized that it was nothing more than foolishness that appealed to the appetites of those whose mouths salivated over sensationalism. I knew that when I was twelve years old!

Unfortunately, some Christians who say they are searching for the truth are merely entertaining the rumors and gossip of tabloid journalism because it is what they want to hear. Some people even promote these stories on social media and other platforms. More often than not, these stories are later proven to be false.

Many of the things promoted at the beginning of 2020 concerning COVID have now been disproven. I witnessed some people removing false stories they posted after being identified as false. I give them credit for removing them; however, they should learn to refrain from posting these false and misleading stories.

I use these recent events as an example of tabloid journalism, and it illustrates what Paul said people would do. He said they would search out those who said what they WANTED to hear. Their truth would be defined by what they desire, not by facts. Their truth would be defined by speculation and feeling rather than corroborating evidence and proof.

This has become a picture of so many today who live in a contrived world based on theory void of facts and evidence. Their baseline of truth is the sensational stories they read on the internet. Even though there is no proof, they continue to believe. They refuse to acknowledge any contrary evidence because the truth no longer matters. Unfortunately, their trust in fabrications has blinded them to the truth.

As Christians, this is not the way we should live. Since the gospel we believe is based on infallible proofs, what we believe about others and the world around us should be likewise. We do not believe things based on floated rumors; we believe because there is evidence supporting the truth. Our entire justice system is based upon this principle. To do anything differently will result in a collapse of our core principles, both natural and spiritual.

Believing a lie is not faith. Rather, it is foolish and void of biblical understanding. The bottom line is if there is no credible evidence to believe something, refuse to accept it. If it cannot be verified, then refuse to promote it. The kingdom of God is based upon undeniable proofs and evidence, which should be the standard for what we believe and promote. Otherwise, we will live in an imaginary world devoid of reality and truth.

At the Root of It All

It is critical to get back to the root cause of this behavior. What causes those who say they have the truth to promote and propagate things that are false? It happens because they listen to a narrative they want to hear and believe is true. In the meantime, the world is watching and concluding that nothing Christians say can be trusted. Some of them justifiably accuse these believers of being crazy.

How can we ever expect the world to believe the gospel we preach as truth while we are promoting false narratives on social media at the same time? The general rule is that if you do not assuredly know something is true beyond any reasonable doubt, it is best not to talk about or share it. Likewise, it is best to refrain from sharing stories published on social media platforms that are not from reliable peer-reviewed sources.

Most of the stories we read on social media platforms come from outlets with little to no accountability. Many of them are debunked quickly, yet they still get traction with those who want to believe them. Again, they WANT to believe it.

It can be agreed that almost all media outlets will report and editorialize with their own bias, but there is at least some measure of accountability with the more prominent ones. Still, this does not guarantee that what is reported is the whole truth, but it does ensure that blatant fabrications are not going to be the regular course of the day. This is not an endorsement for national news media outlets; it is merely a recognition that outlets with no accountability are more likely to contain fabrications, exaggerations, and misleading information.

Historically, some of the most outlandish stories have been promoted through conspiracy theories. Yet, these theories find traction because many people want to believe them. There is such an appetite for sensationalism in the Church (particularly the Charismatic/Prophetic camp) that people latch on to these narratives and promote them as the Word of the Lord, literally a prophetic declaration. To say this is dangerous is a great understatement. However, I have seen countless ministers and believers do this very thing over the last several years, articulating unproven conspiracy theories as a word from the very throne of God. These kinds of things must stop.

Mistaken Spiritual Identity

Throughout my life, I've found that most conspiracy theories never happen. Likewise, I have discovered many things that people ascribe to the voice of the Lord were never uttered by

Him. It seems that many well-meaning believers fall into the trap of authentic desire to hear from the Lord combined with their desire to hear a particular narrative. This causes what I call "mistaken spiritual identity." The voice they desire to hear is mistaken as the prophetic voice of the Lord.

For years, I have heard different ministers say that God revealed to them things concerning the end times. I have also been alive long enough to hear numerous ministers label over a dozen individuals as "The Antichrist," with most having some measure of political power. But many of them died before having an opportunity to take over the world, and some lost their seat of power and will never be able to do what the prognosticators said.

Unfortunately, many believers latch on to these tidbits of supposed revelation and believe them to be prophetic in nature. I would encourage everyone to refrain from believing anything solely because someone says that the Lord showed or told them. Paul commanded that any prophetic word, vision, dream, or visitation must be judged and evaluated by the measuring stick of the Word of God and the witness of the Holy Spirit.

The reality is that the majority of those making false prognostications will not acknowledge their mistake after it fails to materialize. When their proclaimed Antichrist dies without accomplishing anything that was foretold, the minister will pretend nothing was ever said. These things transpiring in the name of the Lord need to stop once and for all because it brings needless reproach upon the Church.

Prophetic Ministry Based on Desire

This same principle can carry over to the lives and ministries of prophets and prophetic people. They can desire to hear something so earnestly until they hear a voice speaking it, but it's the voice of their own desire. Doing this begins to affect what they prophesy because they can hear nothing contrary; the voice of their own desire shouts so loudly that it deafens them to the voice of the Lord.

Many prophets brought about much confusion over the last several years because of words prophesied that never materialized. I understand that some prophetic words are fulfilled in ways different from what we may envision. However, when a word is very specific concerning dates, times, persons, or places, yet fails to happen in that manner, we must conclude that the prophet misspoke.

I equally recognize that all prophecies are conditional whether conditions are stated when given. Yet, if someone gives a specific prophetic word about the end of a pandemic by a certain date or someone winning a particular election by a landslide, its failure to be fulfilled cannot honestly be attributed to unbelief in the lives of those who heard the word. Neither should a prophet "double-down" on their prophetic word when it is obviously wrong. These things only make a bad situation worse.

At the root of these prophetic utterances are the voices that one wants to hear. Someone can desire something to be true or happen so strongly that they can only hear voices of agreement in both the spirit and natural realms. Their desired outcome in a situation becomes so overwhelming that they conjure

VOICES 2

something from their own spiritual well. I will speak more about this in the next chapter.

Your Desire and Prophetic Insight

I have seen ministers prophesy from the place of desire. Their desire was not necessarily a bad thing, but we can never mistake our desire for accurate prophetic insight. They are not the same. Prophets and prophetic people make a big mistake by taking what they desire to happen, speaking that it will happen, and then put "thus says the Lord" at the end. We must discern the voices we hear clearly and recognize that our desire and earnest prayer for something to happen does not equate to God saying it will happen. Ascribing God's name to our desire will not cause it to be fulfilled.

We can be led astray when we become mere echoes of the voices we want to hear. Many times, what we want is not what we need. We may be convinced that our desire is the best thing, but God may have a different idea. It is crucial to recognize that everything we want to hear is not necessarily the voice of the Lord. The voice we long to hear can often be the voice of our own fleshly desire. We must discern correctly.

The Voice of Social Media

Social media outlets of all sorts have become popular with the masses. As a result, Christians spend a tremendous amount of time on different platforms today. When social media first came on the scene, it seemed to be a way to connect, share photos, and reacquaint with others. Instead, it has become a platform for arguments and debates over ideology and current events.

78

Social media platforms are not inherently evil. However, some people have used them in a corrupt manner. Social media is a public platform for whatever is in a person's heart. Out of the abundance of the heart, the mouth will speak, and the fingers will post. These platforms give voice to the hearts and minds of men and women. In times of adversity, when the squeeze is on, the contents of people's hearts are brought to the surface and displayed. I have been shocked and surprised at some of the things I have witnessed.

People have used social media to spew all sorts of vitriol and venom. It has been exploited for all kinds of vile things that are unbecoming of Christians. Unfortunately, many believers have engaged in these behaviors. Even worse, some ministers have done the same things and set a horrible example for others to follow.

If you do not know that something is true, then refuse to post or repeat it. If it cannot be verified by reliable sources, keep it to yourself. How will the world ever believe the truth of the gospel that we claim to preach if we post untrue things on social media?

The Solution Is the Gospel

One solution to this Church problem is a return to the gospel. I am convinced that the Church must get back to the Bible. We are called to preach the gospel, not the latest tabloid story. We are called to meet the needs of humanity through the power of the Holy Spirit. We are commissioned to encourage and edify rather than frighten and alarm. We are called to preach and proclaim the truth of the Word rather than the opinions of man and our own desire or political leaning.

Much of this nonsense would stop if Christians spent more time in the Word than on social media. Unfortunately, the constant appetite for tabloid journalism has given rise to these false voices in the earth because there is an article or story on the internet that will validate whatever you want to believe. There are voices to confirm anything and everything one wants to hear, even though it may be false.

Today, it is imperative that we do not fall into the trap of following false voices. We must rid ourselves of unbiblical biases and allegiances that cause us to hear incorrectly. The voice that one wants to hear is not necessarily the voice of truth. Let us be sensitive to the voice of the Holy Spirit and disallow counterfeit voices from leading us down the road of error.

A Prophetic Dream

Not long ago, I had a prophetic dream. In this dream, I was at the church where my wife and I pastor, High Praise Panama City. I was standing on the platform and proclaimed, "Jesus saves, heals, and delivers." I kept repeating that statement. As I did, I saw the doors of the church building swing open, and people began to come into the building. The more I said it, greater numbers of people came through the doors.

I then had everyone in the congregation stand and instructed them to say in unison, "Jesus saves, heals, and delivers." We all joined in and repeated the phrase over and over. As we all did this together repeatedly, an overwhelming amount of people began to rush through the doors of the church building. I then awoke from the dream.

I sincerely believe that there is a call for the Church to return to preaching and proclaiming the fundamental message of the gospel of Jesus Christ: He saves, heals, and delivers. We must once again let that be the message heard from pulpits across the nation and throughout the world. I believe that great revival will take place, and restoration will be manifested as we do so. So let us purge the articulations of man's theories from the pulpits and return to preaching the gospel. We must refuse to be moved by the voices we want to hear and be led by the voice of the Holy Spirit.

VOICES 2

6

POLLUTED WELLS

"For a good tree does not bear bad fruit, nor does a bad tree bear good fruit. For every tree is known by its own fruit. For men do not gather figs from thorns, nor do they gather grapes from a bramble bush. A good man out of the good treasure of his heart brings forth good; and an evil man out of the evil treasure of his heart brings forth evil. For out of the abundance of the heart his mouth speaks" (Luke 6:43-45).

This Scripture is a familiar passage that most Christians have heard repeatedly. However, we have mainly heard only the last portion of these verses, "For out of the abundance of the heart, his mouth will speak." I want to focus on this all-important principle that Jesus articulated.

Jesus said that when someone has good treasure in their heart, they will bring forth or say good things. Contrastingly, when someone has evil treasure in their heart, they will bring forth or say evil things. The mouth is merely a reflection of what is in the heart. Hence, the determining factor of whether something coming out of the mouth is good or evil is the contents of the heart. If the deposit inside someone's heart is good and godly, their words will also be good and godly. If the deposit inside someone's heart is polluted, then their words will be likewise. The purity of a voice is determined by the contents of the heart.

The Well of the Heart

The heart of man is like a well—a place from where water is drawn. When Jesus met the woman at the well of Samaria, he said the water He would give was like a "well of water springing up" (John 4:14). That well of water springs up from the heart of someone who is born again. Jesus went further to say that the Holy Spirit would flow like "rivers of living water."

The water that Jesus spoke of flows from the heart or spirit of man. It is the place where the Holy Spirit dwells within a Christian. At the time of salvation, a well of life is generated. When someone is filled with the Holy Spirit, it becomes a flowing river of living water. This is what Jesus said would take place.

However, just as wells and rivers can be polluted naturally, they can also be polluted in the spirit. It is possible for someone who is saved and Spirit-filled to pollute the spiritual well of their heart. Different things can pollute the flow of our hearts, which we will discuss in more detail. We must first understand that our spiritual wells can become contaminated and polluted based on what we deposit within them.

We have established that the heart or spirit of man is likened to a well. We have also confirmed that out of the abundance of the well of the heart, the mouth will speak. So, the contents of the well (heart) determine whether a voice is pure or polluted.

If someone watches over the well of their heart to keep it clean and pure, their voice will be clean and pure. If they have allowed their well (heart) to be contaminated or polluted, their voice will be contaminated and polluted.

"Keep your heart with all diligence, for out of it is the wellspring of life. Put away from yourself a perverse mouth. Put corrupt lips far from you" (Proverbs 4:23-24, WEBP).

Here we see the importance of keeping our hearts pure and free from spiritual contamination. The Hebrew word translated "keep" means *to guard*. Some translations read, "Guard your heart." God has given us the responsibility of guarding what goes into our hearts. It is imperative that we keep our hearts and spirits pure. If we fail to do so, it will negatively influence what is coming out of our mouths. If our hearts are impure, the words of our mouths will be impure. If our inner man is contaminated, our voice will spew the same thing.

After the instruction to guard our hearts, there is the directive to put away a perverse mouth. It is important to understand that these two things are inherently connected. If we fail to guard our hearts, we will have a perverse mouth—a polluted voice. However, if we guard our hearts and maintain purity, we will not have perverse mouths and corrupt lips. This is true because out of the abundance of the heart, the mouth will speak. The voice reflects what is in the heart.

"A righteous man who falters before the wicked is like a murky spring and a polluted well" (Proverbs 25:26).

In this verse, we see that things happen when a righteous person (someone saved) falls into sinful behavior. It says they become like a polluted well; the well of their heart becomes contaminated through ungodly conduct. It can also be polluted by entertaining things that are worldly, carnal, false, or hateful. Therefore, we must be careful what we read, hear, and watch because it is a major aspect of guarding our hearts. We must refuse to allow anything into our hearts that could possibly contaminate our spiritual wells.

Many things can pollute the well of someone's heart. Sinful living, fleshly behavior, constant hearing of false theories, ungodly biases, negative speaking, slander, maliciousness, idolatry, and man-worship are a few things that can severely pollute your well. When someone engages in these behaviors, it causes their voice to be polluted and then defiles those who hear them.

Pulpits Must Remain Unpolluted

To those who occupy pulpits and are tasked with preaching the gospel, it is imperative that we guard our hearts against all the aforementioned things. We must keep ourselves pure and holy before God and disallow these things from entering our hearts. If there is a constant deposit of impure things within our lives, our voices will become corrupted, and it will be heard in our preaching, teaching, and prophesying. Yes, even prophetic words can become polluted when the heart of the one prophesying is contaminated with the wrong things.

Over the last several years, I have heard many outlandish things come out of the mouths of ministers of the gospel. Prophetic words were given that were inaccurate because they were polluted with bias, political partisanship, and division, along with the voice they wanted to hear. Some pastors used their pulpits to vent their hate for those with whom they disagreed. Social media pages of ministers became the whipping post for those that did not agree with their opinion on the COVID virus. These actions happened because of contaminated wells. The pollution of the opinions and theories of man, with no biblical basis, infected the hearts of many.

Voices from polluted wells posed as the authentic prophetic word of the Lord. However, the word that was delivered did not meet the litmus test of Scripture. One could easily discern that the motivation was not to promote the testimony of Jesus but rather to promote a particular disposition and leaning. Those who had similar feelings cheered because it was the voice they wanted to hear. Those who possessed untainted spiritual wells recognized it for what it was.

"The mouth of the righteous is a well of life, But violence covers the mouth of the wicked. Hatred stirs up strife, But love covers all sins" (Proverbs 10:11-12).

Many Christians and ministers have promoted doctrines of hate in recent years. Although it has always been present in some circles, things went beyond disagreement and crossed over to verbal personal attacks against those who thought differently. Of course, people will always have differing opinions about a myriad of things, and they can debate these things in a civil manner. However, I have heard some people take things to a level that I have never witnessed in my time here on earth and in ministry.

The hatred and vitriol coming from believers' mouths revealed a deep problem in the underbelly of the Church. Voices listened to by many were filled with hatred, slander, and maliciousness. The result was evident in believers' hearts that became contaminated and polluted and then echoed the same hate, disdain, and division. Long-standing relationships were severed because many Christians allowed their own well to be polluted by the voices of those who already possessed polluted wells. It became an endless circle: polluted wells, polluted voices, polluted wells, and polluted voices.

A Strong Word Calling for Change

I recognize that this is a strong word, but if we do not realize what happened and is happening, we will continue down the same path of destruction. **There is a cry of the Spirit today for repentance and change.** If we persist in listening to voices filled with hatred and slander, our hearts and wells will be filled with the same. Then our voices will become polluted like the ones to whom we are listening. It is just that simple. The solution is to cut off that polluted voice in your life. You must guard your heart because out of it will flow the issues of life. Out of the abundance of your heart, your mouth will speak.

We can disagree with someone without being disagreeable and spiteful. My wife and I have been married for over 40 years and are total opposites. We disagree on many things and let each other know. However, we refuse to hate one another because of disagreement over nonessential issues. We refuse to allow those things to separate and alienate us, which can only be accomplished when hearts are filled with love and appreciation for one another.

If our hearts are pure with the love of God, that is what will proceed from our mouths. If our hearts are contaminated with hatred and slander, then that is what will flow from our mouths. The latter will result in strife, division, discord, backbiting, and every evil thing under the sun.

It is interesting that the previous Scripture states the mouth of the righteous is a well of life. Every Christian should desire for their mouth be that kind of well. This happens when the well of your heart is filled with life. If it is filled with other things, that is what will be voiced. If we fill our hearts with hatred, our voices will reflect the same and stir up strife. If our hearts are filled with love, our voices will cover sin and prevent it from being reproduced, just as the Scripture declares.

Sin That Dulls Your Hearing

Sin, by its very nature, is deceptive. Therefore, the practice of sinful and ungodly behavior will open the door for the voice of deception. It allows this voice to establish a stronghold in the lives of those it victimizes. The more someone continues to sin willfully, the greater the stronghold this voice will establish. The end of this is that one is convinced the voice of deception is the voice of truth.

Repeated dabbling and practice of sin will keep the door open for one to be deceived. The voice of deception will ultimately convince them that their sinful activity is virtuous and acceptable. This error results in them believing that the sin they are committing has God's stamp of approval. The Bible refers to this as a "seared conscience."

> Now the Spirit expressly says that in latter times some will depart from the faith, giving heed to deceiving spirits and doctrines of demons, speaking lies in hypocrisy, having

their own conscience seared with a hot iron (1
Timothy 4:1-2).

Notice the progression in this passage of Scripture. First, they
heed deceiving spirits (voices) which promote doctrines of
demons. Secondly, they echo these things by speaking
hypocritical lies and falsehoods. Lastly, their conscience is
seared with a hot iron. Wow! Draw your own conclusions as to
how we have witnessed the application of this Scripture in our
present culture and society.

This is the spiritual progression that takes place. There is first
the entertaining of voices of deception. People give their ear
over to voices originating from polluted wells—the voices they
want to hear even if they are filled with lies. Then, they begin
to echo the things they have heard, allowing their well to be
polluted with lies. Ultimately, they believe the lie is the truth,
and it results in a seared conscience. When this happens, the
voice of truth and conviction has no ability to penetrate the
heart. Their ear to truth is deaf and, therefore, cannot receive
it because of a seared conscience that is no longer sensitive to
God's voice. This scenario is very dangerous.

Balaam the Madman

Many of us are familiar with the account of the prophet
Balaam. He was a man called to be the mouthpiece of the Lord
and lead God's people down the road of righteousness. The
Bible clearly states that Balaam put a stumbling block in front
of the Israelites that caused them to sin. He did the exact
opposite of what God called and ordained him to do and
accomplish.

Balaam was to be the voice of the Lord to those who had no ability to hear it. He was there to declare the way of the Lord and command God's people to walk in that manner; however, he failed to do so. He never prophesied anything inaccurately, yet he is recognized as a false prophet. One of the things that made him false was the sin and iniquity in his heart, which then caused him to lose his ability to hear and see correctly. His well was polluted.

> They have forsaken the right way and gone astray, following the way of Balaam the son of Beor, who loved the wages of unrighteousness; but he was rebuked for his iniquity: a dumb donkey speaking with a man's voice restrained the madness of the prophet. These are wells without water, clouds carried by a tempest, for whom is reserved the blackness of darkness forever. For when they speak great swelling words of emptiness, they allure through the lusts of the flesh, through lewdness, the ones who have actually escaped from those who live in error (2 Peter 2:15-18).

Peter refers to the prophet as a madman—a crazy person. On the heels of this, Peter says explicitly, "These are wells without water." The analogy given portrays the mad prophet as a well with no water. He could no longer deliver anything life-giving to those God called him to minister. He no longer had any life-sustaining water. Balaam had nothing but pollution and contamination in his well. He allowed the lust for money and power to pollute his well.

The fact that Balaam would even consider Balak's offer indicated that he allowed things to crowd into his heart and contaminate his spirit. His heart had become so polluted that he could not see straight. The donkey he was riding had more spiritual insight than him. His well was contaminated and caused him to be spiritually blind, deaf, and undiscerning of his situation.

The contamination in his well had become so great that he became a madman. The word translated as "madness" literally means *insanity*. The prophet became insane in his actions and deeds. I believe this insanity was fostered by the fact that he allowed spiritual contamination and pollution to overtake his well, the well of his heart.

Contamination of Idols Breed Insanity

In Numbers 22, we find the account of Balaam riding his donkey to meet Balak, the king who wanted him to curse the Israelites. An angel of the Lord stood with a sword to prevent Balaam and the donkey from passing. The donkey saw the angel, but Balaam did not. This happened three times, and each time Balaam went into a fit of rage and struck the donkey.

The final time, the donkey collapsed under Balaam. So, he took his rod and beat the donkey. God opened the mouth of the donkey, and he asked Balaam why he was beating him. Here is the amazing thing, Balaam talked back to the donkey. It is somewhat comical to envision the story as you read; it is like a scene from an animated movie.

Think about this for a moment. Balaam could not see the angel while the donkey could see him clearly. Not once or twice did this happen, but three times. The donkey had never been known to speak, but Balaam carried on an entire dialogue with the beast of burden like it was a common occurrence with no shock or surprise. This event shows how far things had gone downhill in the life of the prophet.

Balaam was anointed to prophesy, but his well had become so filled with spiritual pollution that he was unable to recognize what was happening. He was blind to the angel standing with a sword; he was blind to the fact that an animal was talking; he was blind to the fact that he was responding and carrying on a conversation with a beast of burden. This is where sin's contamination had taken Balaam; he became a madman and acted insanely.

Prophetic Craziness

A few prophets that I heard prophesy in the last decade fit into this same category, madmen. The things they said bordered on insanity. Some of it was so crazy that there were no words to describe it. Their wells were polluted, and they became madmen. The words they spoke, while labeled prophetic, were nothing but craziness.

I am not calling anyone a false prophet, but I am saying that pollution and contamination caused many to say inappropriate things that God was not saying. I personally believe that most of this stemmed from biases and preconceptions they believed to be the voice of the Lord. However, these things will pollute spiritual wells and cause presumptuous prophecies.

In the life of Balaam, the entertainment of sin and iniquity caused him to be blind to what a donkey could see. When people allow their wells to become contaminated in this manner, others can see what they cannot. There is a dullness that prevents them from seeing and hearing correctly. **They believe they are right, while those who are spiritually discerning can see they are wrong. Think about it!**

An Impure Heart Seeks the Wrong Things

There must have been something present within the heart of Balaam that possessed him to seek after Balak. The prophet was not required to give him audience; he could have easily said that the offer was repulsive and abominable. However, he did none of these things.

Some have speculated it was greed in the heart of Balaam. Some have said it was acceptance and popularity. Others have floated the idea that political power and influence became his motivation. I personally agree with all of them. I would even say that it was not one or the other, but possibly a combination of all these factors. But, that is only my opinion.

Balaam had an itch that he desired to be scratched. He wanted money, power, acceptance, and fame. This is not some new strategy the enemy utilizes on prophets. These are the same things that the devil has historically used on those whom he leads astray. He still uses this strategy today.

Balaam's heart was polluted by fleshly desires; his uncontrolled urges and dispositions made him insane. The voice of the flesh became so loud in his life that he could no longer hear the voice of the Lord. He lost his ability to spiritually see and discern to the point that a beast of burden had greater insight than him. His uncontrolled urges and dispositions drove him insane. The anointed man of God became less sensitive in the spirit than a donkey. As a result, the prophet became a madman.

Can we all take an introspective look today? Can we all examine ourselves to see if we have allowed things to crowd our hearts and contaminate our spiritual wells? Can we be honest before God and ask Him to reveal and remove anything that may cause us to walk the same path as Balaam? If we will, God will be faithful to reveal and remove these things from our lives.

VOICES 2

7

BEWARE OF IDOLS

"Son of man, these men have set up their idols in their hearts, and put before them that which causes them to stumble into iniquity. Should I let Myself be inquired of at all by them? Therefore speak to them, and say to them, 'Thus says the Lord GOD: "Everyone of the house of Israel who sets up his idols in his heart, and puts before him what causes him to stumble into iniquity, and then comes to the prophet, I the LORD will answer him who comes, according to the multitude of his idols, that I may seize the house of Israel by their heart, because they are all estranged from Me by their idols.""" (Ezekiel 14:3-5).

This passage of Scripture has always been controversial for those who embrace the prophetic ministry in the Church. Especially as it pertains to what God says He will do to the prophet who prophesies according to the idols of one's heart. I would like to primarily focus on an issue that causes hearts to be contaminated and polluted, resulting in inaccurate or false prophetic words. That issue is idolatry.

The sin of idolatry will not only negatively affect anyone receiving prophetic ministry but also the individual ministering the word. Idols within the heart of a believer cause them to hear incorrectly because their wells are polluted. It causes prophets and prophetic ministers to speak falsely because they have a contaminated source from where they are drawing water, their own hearts.

When someone has an idol in their heart, they will seek to hear a word that confirms and condones the idol they possess. When someone prophesies with an idol in their heart, the word given will confirm and condone the idol in their own heart. This is the bottom line: **People will hear and speak according to idols in their hearts.** The polluted heart will spew words that are polluted.

Polluted with Idols

Throughout the Bible, God repeatedly speaks of those who pollute themselves with idols. When anyone allows a thing or person to assume a place in their life that is designated for the Lord only, they are committing the sin of idolatry. If there are ideas, biases, and leanings that have been exalted in their life that are not subject to the authority of God's Word, it becomes an idol. Things one cannot separate themself from, which are ungodly and unbiblical, become objects of idolatry within their heart. These idols contaminate and pollute the hearts and minds of man.

When one thinks of an idol, they often think of something like a totem pole around which a tribal people might dance. However, an idol is not a Tiki doll purchased in Honolulu that sits on your mantle. Idols are thoughts, ideas, beliefs, individuals, biases, and leanings that someone holds dear, which they refuse to give up because of the exalted place it has in their heart. Things such as these are usually unbiblical and fail to pass the test of Bible accuracy and congruence. These are the things that pollute the well of the heart and prevent our voice from being pure. Remember, Jesus said that the mouth will speak what is in the heart. If there are idols in one's heart, that is what will be given voice.

> Woe to her who is rebellious and polluted, To the oppressing city! She has not obeyed His voice, She has not received correction; She has not trusted in the LORD, She has not drawn near to her God... Her prophets are insolent, treacherous people; Her priests have polluted the sanctuary, They have done violence to the law (Zephaniah 3:1-2, 4).

It is interesting how the Lord draws a connection between rebellion, pollution, and discarding His voice. These three things seem always to be found in the same heap. Wherever you find one, you will always find the others.

These Scripture verses specifically point out that the ministers, prophets, and priests polluted the sanctuary. Transitioning this verse into a New Testament application, we recognize that the sanctuary of the Lord is the heart of man. The Holy Spirit now dwells within the heart of those who are born-again, those who are saved. We see that **God's sanctuary, the heart of the believer, can be polluted and defiled by the very ones tasked with ministering to God's people. Think about it.**

Again, when ministers have idols in their hearts, it will pollute the hearts of many. When prophets allow their wells to be contaminated by their own ideas, opinions, and theories, it will also affect the hearts of others. Instead of ministering life, they will be the spewers of false stories, human ideology, and theories from their self-created fantasy land. They will say, "Thus says the Lord…" when God is not saying it at all. However, ascribing the name of the Lord to a word from a polluted well will not make it true nor come to pass.

No Lines of Communication

The prophet Ezekiel said Israel was "all estranged from [God] by their idols" (Ezekiel 14:5). Remember, he is speaking to God's covenant people. It is typical with estranged relationships that there is no communication. There is usually something that caused division and separation which prevents them from talking to one another. The lines of communication are broken and severed in estrangement.

God said that idols within the heart cause communication to be cut off. Believers cannot hear the voice of the Lord accurately when there are idols within their hearts. A prophet's voice will be inaccurate if he has an idol in his heart because he has alienated himself from the Lord. With his gifting, he may prophesy, but the word will usually be filled with contaminated water.

> "For My people have committed two evils: They have forsaken Me, the fountain of living waters, And hewn themselves cisterns—broken cisterns that can hold no water" (Jeremiah 2:13).

The Lord says His people have forsaken the living water and made their own wells. The first evil or sin is the decision to leave the fountain of living water. The second sin is to create and fabricate a well to their liking that has no ability to hold water for refreshing or nourishment.

Not What I Wanted to Hear

I have seen people seek out a prophetic word. When the word came to them, they decided they did not like or appreciate it. The word was not what they wanted to hear. So, they decided to go to someone else to get another word, hoping they would receive what they desired. They forsook the fountain of living water because they did not like its taste.

I recall in the earlier days of my ministry, when I was on staff with a leading national prophetic ministry, on a particular occasion I was asked to prophesy to people who had come to a conference we hosted. I ministered to them what I sensed the Lord was saying. Unfortunately, they did not like the word I gave to them. So, they went to the ministry's leaders and expressed their displeasure with my prophetic ability. In their minds, I had certainly missed it. This resulted in one of our leaders ministering prophetically to them without any knowledge of what I had prophesied. The word he prophesied was almost verbatim to what I had ministered to them. They were upset and left the conference. Why did they do that? It was because they did not like the water coming out of the fountain.

This event is an example of how people can forsake the fountain of living water because they do not like what it is pouring out. It is not the flavor they want, so they seek a different one elsewhere. The word they receive does not fit their liking, so they decide to create their own well that can hold no water, but it will be what they like. This takes us to the next evil spoken about by the Lord.

Fabrication of Wells

Being unappreciative of what God is pouring out within our lives is not a good thing. However, when we take it to the next level and attempt to create and fabricate a well that only He can fashion, we assume that we know what we need better than the Lord Himself. That behavior is a manifestation of pride and arrogance. It is the statement that we possess abilities to fabricate something greater than what God can create.

Notice that the Lord said they had hewn out cisterns and wells for themselves. Instead of a God-ordained and God-fashioned fountain of living water, they made a counterfeit well that had no ability even to contain water. They substituted the holy with the profane. They replaced the clean with the contaminated. Fabricating your own well shuts out the true living water.

Unfortunately, this can happen within the lives and ministries of any five-fold ministry gift. When idols form in the hearts of ministers, they will create and fabricate their own well that God did not fashion. It will look like a godly well from external appearances but contain no life-giving water. It may gush with their own opinions and fleshly doctrines, yet it will not gush with a flow from heaven. It may even look tantalizing, glitzy, and appetizing on the outside, but it will not quench the spiritual thirst and longing of the hearts of God's people. The bottom line is that an illegitimate counterfeit well is created that becomes the residence of the idols of their heart.

> Now it came to pass when the king was dwelling in his house, and the LORD had given him rest from all his enemies all around, that the king said to Nathan the prophet, "See now, I dwell in a house of cedar, but the ark of God dwells inside tent curtains." Then Nathan said to the king, "Go, do all that is in your heart, for the LORD is with you." But it happened that night that the word of the LORD came to Nathan, saying, "Go and tell My servant David, 'Thus says the LORD: "Would you build a house for Me to dwell in?..."' 'When your days are fulfilled and you rest with your fathers, I will set up your seed after you, who will come from your body, and I will establish his kingdom. He shall build a house for My name, and I will establish the throne of his kingdom forever'" (2 Samuel 7:1-5, 12-13).

In this account, the prophet Nathan speaks something to David presumptuously. It was understood when the king came to the prophet that whatever the prophet said was the word of the Lord. This was not merely a casual conversation between King David and the prophet Nathan.

David wanted to do a good thing; he wanted to build the house of the Lord. Nathan responded to the king's desire and longing with affirmation. He told David to go and do what was in his heart. Furthermore, he said, "The Lord is with you." Not only did Nathan give the king the green light to proceed, but he also proclaimed that God was with him in this venture.

In this account, the prophet was giving specific direction to the king. David sought out divine guidance for a plan that he had in his heart to accomplish. Nathan, as a prophet, spoke two things inaccurately. The first was for David to go ahead with his plan to build the house of the Lord. The second was that God was involved in his plan to build. Neither thing was true.

God spoke to Nathan later in the evening and told him that he had missed it. The word of the Lord was that David was not to build the house of the Lord; instead, his seed would be charged with that responsibility after David was no longer alive on the earth. So, the accurate word of the Lord was that God was not with David in his plan to begin a construction project.

I believe it shows great humility in the life and ministry of Nathan that he would return to the king to correct the error he made. He was willing to say, *"Respectfully, King, I missed it yesterday."* Wow! Unfortunately, there seem to be very few prophets willing to do that today. It appears we live in the "double down" era of prophetic ministry. The humility that Nathan displayed needs to return to prophets and prophetic people today. No prophet should ever claim infallibility. Nathan did not, and neither should any prophet today!

The Subtleness of Allegiances

The thing that I am most interested in us observing from this entire account of Nathan and David is the dynamic that motivated the prophet to speak inaccurately. Nathan had a great record of accurate prophetic ministry. He was the one who confronted David when he sinned with Bathsheba and had her husband Uriah killed. It is obvious that Nathan loved

David; he was loyal to the king and would never do anything to mislead him deliberately. Nathan recognized his responsibility and was willing to say whatever the Lord spoke to him without fear. So, what would cause him to say and prophesy something presumptuously?

I believe what led to Nathan's mistake was he let his personal loyalty and allegiance to the king momentarily hinder his judgment and prophetic accuracy. I believe it could also be stated that **David had a strong desire to build the house of the Lord, and it became an exalted thing within his life, possibly an idol in his own heart. Think about it.**

Loyalty is a wonderful trait for any individual, providing it is held in check. However, any unbridled allegiance to anyone will lead them down a road of error that can lead to idolatry and the forfeiture of accurate discernment. Nathan's allegiance to David had become a stumbling block to his precise hearing. Instead of clearly hearing the voice of the Lord, the voice of allegiance spoke louder.

Let me break this down to where the rubber meets the road. Nathan had a political allegiance with the king. Rather than speaking the unadulterated word of the Lord to those in power, he allowed his allegiance to form his declaration. His loyalty was not necessarily evil. However, the moment his allegiance was exalted, it became a hindrance. His loyalty and allegiance in an unbridled state prevented him from speaking accurately. His voice was contaminated by an exalted allegiance.

The Interference of Allegiance

The unfortunate truth is that when any minister of the gospel forms allegiances based on personal biases and preferences, it has the potential to interfere with their ability to speak accurately. This is because allegiance can contaminate the well of the heart. There is a very fine line between biblical loyalty and an exalted allegiance that turns to idolatry. Unfortunately, far too many people cross that thin line without the knowledge they are doing so.

Some ministers will say, "*I would never do that.*" I am sure Nathan never thought it possible that his allegiance to David would interfere with accurate ministry. However, it did. This devotion is the danger zone that so many have wandered into unknowingly. The unfortunate thing that is ongoing today is there are fewer prophets and ministers who have the humility of Nathan and are willing to admit their mistakes.

Blind allegiance to anyone or anything is very dangerous. It can be attributed to some of the most heinous historical atrocities. Dictators of evil empires were given power because of blind allegiances. Populous allegiance and loyalties have enabled the worst rulers to carry out their desires without any resistance. Adolph Hitler is a prime example. This danger is the reason it is so important that Christians and ministers ensure that any loyalty they possess does not become an idol within their hearts.

I am not saying these things to accuse or condemn anyone. However, I believe it is important for us to be introspective and examine ourselves, especially those of us who claim prophetic giftings. We must steward the grace of God in purity and refuse to allow our prophetic well to be tainted.

Biblical Values

I believe the Church is called to affect every realm of society and culture, including the area of government. Therefore, every believer should possess beliefs and values based on Scripture, the Word of God. These values transcend political parties and platforms. They are not exclusively owned by any specific political organization.

So, the values to which we ascribe as Christians are not exclusively owned by any specific political party or organization. Our values should be rooted in biblical principles, which means our first loyalty and allegiance is to Jesus and His kingdom.

For instance, I believe that abortion is wrong and that babies have a right to live, but that does not in itself make me a Republican. I believe that we should take care of widows and orphans along with providing aid and assistance to them, but that does not make me a Democrat. I believe we should be good stewards of the earth within reason and plausibility, but that does not make me part of the Green Party. These are all biblical values that may be associated with one party to a greater degree but are not exclusively owned by them. These values are derived from the Bible.

Our First Allegiance

My first and foremost allegiance is to Jesus and His kingdom; I will only follow a man to the degree that he follows Christ. The apostle Paul instructed Corinthian believers to follow him as he followed Christ (1 Corinthians 11:1). This same principle would apply to anyone who could be a potential governmental leader, from the President to the dog catcher. My political loyalty to them goes only as far as their commitment to follow Christ. The moment they cease to follow Jesus in word or deed, I cease to follow them.

It is interesting to note that the Jews who cried out for Jesus to be crucified possessed a political idol. When Jesus stood before Pilate, the chief priests cried, "We have no king but Caesar!" (John 19:15). Amazingly, they possessed allegiance to the Roman Empire but none to Jesus and His kingdom. Could it be that their unbridled allegiance to a natural political power caused them to see and hear incorrectly and miss the Messiah? **Could it be that their loyalty to an emperor caused them to cry out for the crucifixion of the very Son of God? Think about it.**

A Deceptive Issue

Allegiances to political candidates and parties are one of the most deceptive issues facing the Church. The reason I say that is because some Christians equate supporting a politician to following God. There are believers who have stated that promoting a particular politician and political party means that you are on God's side, regardless of how those politicians or parties conduct themselves.

I have heard numerous ministers say that a Christian's love and loyalty to God were measured by their allegiance to a specific politician. I was shocked by these statements. However, many Christians cheered for these ministers because it was what they wanted to hear declared. The words they spoke pacified the idol they possessed in their own heart.

Statements that equate our love of God to political positions are heretical. The marriage of Christianity to American politics on both sides of the aisle has produced undesirable things in the Church that need to be corrected. We must consider our ways and allow the Holy Spirit to bring adjustment and correction.

What Did Jesus Do?

Is the litmus test of our love for God now determined by political leanings and how one votes in a democratic election? Is holy and righteous living no longer a determining factor? Is loving our neighbor no longer an indicator of someone's love for the Lord? What has taken the Church down this path? Blind political allegiances have produced this problem and have formed idols within the hearts of many Christians. May God help us!

Jesus nor His disciples were loyal to the Scribes, Pharisees, Herod, or Caesar. The apostle Paul indicated no political allegiances in any of his writings. We are called to influence every realm of society, but we should never equate a political allegiance to one's dedication and love for the Lord. This kind of action is divisive and dangerous. I may not agree with someone's political stand, but if they are saved, they are my fellow member of the body of Christ.

Since U. S. citizens live in a democratic republic, we can vote for candidates of our choosing. There is nothing evil or wrong with supporting the candidate you believe will do the best job. As Christians, we should desire to see godly people with godly character, who support biblical values, placed in office, and we should vote accordingly. However, an unbridled allegiance that equates political support to loyalty to God is dangerous. It can become an idol in the heart that will give voice to inaccurate and presumptuous declarations.

As an American citizen, one is free to support the political candidate of their choice. Look at Paul's qualifications for elders and deacons as a good place to define what is needed in politicians we choose to support today. However, the moment that someone's allegiance to a candidate is equated to loving God, Jesus is made into nothing more than a politician. Christianity then becomes merely a political party and position. This ideology is antithetical to everything taught in the Bible, specifically the New Testament.

I want to make it clear that I believe the Church should be involved in political arenas. We are called to be salt and light, affecting every realm of the earth. However, we cannot allow blind allegiances to exist within our hearts because that becomes idolatry. It is vital that Christians vote and uphold biblical values, but we cannot become nasty to others who do not believe the same. Our involvement in politics must be tempered and balanced with an unshakable loyalty to Jesus and His kingdom.

> "An astonishing and horrible thing Has been committed in the land: The prophets prophesy falsely, And the priests rule by their own power; And My people love to have it so. But what will you do in the end?" (Jeremiah 5:30-31).

Jeremiah speaks of a time when the prophets not only speak inaccurately in the name of the Lord, but people love it when they do. This behavior is a trap to which Christians and ministers can fall prey. Believers want to hear a particular narrative preached and declared. The ministers realize if they do not say it, the people will leave and go across town where another person is declaring it. Those with itching ears will gravitate to the voice they want to hear.

Truth May Not Be Popular

Unfortunately, the truth is not often popular. Jesus preached on one occasion, and everyone left except His disciples. Jesus looked at His disciples and asked them if they were going to leave also. Wisely, Peter said there was nowhere else to go because Jesus was the only One with the words of life.

Think about this. The people who left while Jesus was preaching forsook the words of life that had the power to deliver them. The truth was not popular with that group of people. They wanted a prophet to say what they wanted to hear, even if it was false. In leaving, they forfeited their own deliverance.

This same thing happens in the Church. There is a narrative that many believers want to hear or a prophetic word they seek. So they pursue it until they find those who will say what they want to hear. Even if the word is false, they love and embrace the proclamation since it agrees with their predisposition. That is what Jeremiah said happened in his day, and it seems some of the same things are still happening.

The primary issue we have in some prophetic circles today is that some ministers and prophets continue to speak words from polluted spiritual wells while lacking wisdom. If certain wells of the prophetic continue to be filled with improper allegiances and motives, the integrity of prophets and the prophetic word will be compromised. These are the things that must be corrected, balanced, and realigned.

What Will You Do?

An interesting question is asked by the Lord in this passage from Jeremiah, "What will you do in the end?" I sincerely believe that God is proposing this question to the body of Christ. What are we going to do about these things? Will we continue to allow our wells to be polluted? Will we allow idols to dwell in our hearts? Will we allow unchecked allegiances to remain within our hearts and minds? I hope that the answer to all these questions is a resounding "No!"

8

WRONG COUNSEL

Blessed is the man Who walks not in the counsel of the ungodly, Nor stands in the path of sinners, Nor sits in the seat of the scornful; But his delight is in the law of the LORD, And in His law he meditates day and night. He shall be like a tree Planted by the rivers of water, That brings forth its fruit in its season, Whose leaf also shall not wither; And whatever he does shall prosper. The ungodly are not so, But are like the chaff which the wind drives away. Therefore the ungodly shall not stand in the judgment, Nor sinners in the congregation of the righteous. For the LORD knows the way of the righteous, But the way of the ungodly shall perish (Psalm 1:1-6).

This Psalm contrasts the life of the blessed man with the life of the cursed, the godly to the ungodly, and the holy to the unholy. The primary thing that stands out is the difference between the person who lives in God's blessing versus those who are outside of it. There are specific things mentioned which are characteristic in the behavior of the person who lives in the blessing of the Lord, those experiencing the manifestation of God's provision and favor. When these things are enacted within the life of a believer, blessing is inevitable.

It is evident in this Psalm that those who are in covenant with God should live differently. We are called to live a sanctified life before the Lord. We should not act, talk, or behave like those steeped in a worldly and sinful system. There should be a remarkable difference between those who call themselves Christians and those who are unsaved.

The bottom line is that if we look and act like the world, we will forfeit the promised blessing. Although God does not remove it from our lives, our behavior causes a forfeiture. The promise goes unclaimed because ungodly behavior voids its fulfillment.

The Lord makes everything very simple. He declares that living our lives in His prescribed manner will cause a tangible blessing to overtake us. He also says that living contrary to His commands and precepts will cause the same blessing to bypass us. It is just that simple. Obey and be blessed, or disobey and experience the curse. The choice is ours.

God told the Israelites that He put blessing and cursing, life and death before them. He then gave them some excellent counsel: "Choose life, that both you and your descendants may live" (Deuteronomy 30:19). He told them to make the right choice by following His directives.

The First Directive in the First Psalm

The first directive of the very first verse of the very first Psalm is this: Do not listen to ungodly counsel. The Psalmist said that the person who refrains from walking in ungodly counsel would be blessed. Think about this and let it weigh on your heart. The first thing emphasized in the very first verse of the entire book of Psalms is to be careful of what you hear and allow in your heart.

God felt it so important that His people not listen to wrong voices that He made it His first proclamation in the book primarily comprised of songs written by David, the man after God's own heart. Could it be that the heart of God is bent toward His people listening to correct voices? Could He be concerned about the voices to which we listen? I believe that "YES" is the answer to these questions.

God emphasizes that we should not give our ear over to voices that speak ungodly counsel. Instead, He accentuates the need to give our heart and ear to that which is wholesome, godly, and saturated with His Word. Doing so will cause His blessing to abound, whereas failure will cause His desire to be omitted from our lives.

Garbage In, Garbage Out

There is a phrase used in computer science called "garbage in, garbage out." Basically, it means that if you program something with bad information, then it will spit out bad information. This is also a principle of life that applies to everything, including our thinking and believing. Listening to unwise and ungodly counsel produces bad fruit and causes God's blessing to be forfeited.

Many Christians miss out on God's best for their lives solely because they listen to wrong voices. It may be the voice of their friend or neighbor. It could be the voice they long to hear because it pacifies their sinful behavior. However, it is the voice that is regurgitating ungodly and unwise counsel that steers them in the wrong direction. Sadly, I have seen it repeatedly happen in the lives of born-again, Spirit-filled believers.

One of the most dangerous things a believer can do is listen to ungodly counsel. It can wreak pain and havoc in their lives while they believe they are doing the right thing.

Words to Appease

Here is an example of how this works. Someone goes to their friend with a problem they are experiencing. The friend, acting out of what they believe to be genuine care, gives them counsel and a shoulder to cry on. The person with the problem enacts the counsel they received, believing they have found the solution. Unfortunately, nothing changes for the better; things actually get worse, and they are eventually disheartened and devastated.

The problem in this scenario is that the friend who gave counsel only tried to make the troubled individual feel better. They spoke words to appease and placate. However, the counsel they gave was unbiblical and unwise. It contradicted what was right and godly while appealing only to emotions. Instead of making things better, their counsel made things much worse.

The individual who acted on the bad counsel was left in confusion. They believed they listened to good counsel because the person giving the counsel was a Christian. However, they were given nothing but vain words that were powerless in the situation.

It is important to understand that sometimes Christians can counsel people with worldly advice. Saying "yes" to Jesus does not automatically fill someone with the wisdom of God. There is a process of being transformed by the renewing of your mind that must take place. This process is not done overnight; it takes time. Novice believers should not be counseling anyone other than telling the lost they need Jesus.

> Then to Adam He said, "Because you have heeded the voice of your wife, and have eaten from the tree of which I commanded you, saying, 'You shall not eat of it': Cursed is the ground for your sake; In toil you shall eat of it All the days of your life. Both thorns and thistles it shall bring forth for you, And you shall eat the herb of the field. In the sweat of your face you shall eat bread Till you return to the ground, For out of it you were taken; For dust you are, And to dust you shall return." (Genesis 3:17-19).

God expressly declared the root of Adam's sin was that he heeded wrong counsel. He harkened to the voice of his wife. He listened to the wrong voice. Adam should have protected and corrected his wife rather than heeding her instruction. Instead, he walked in ungodly counsel that resulted in the forfeiture of the blessing of the Lord.

Eve sinned because she listened to the voice of the serpent. Adam sinned because he listened to Eve's counsel. **Adam heeded the counsel of someone who listened to the wrong voice. Think about that!**

As a result of Adam heeding ungodly counsel, the curse came into the earth. Adam and Eve lost their home and their possessions, leaving the Garden of Eden with nothing but some souvenir clothing God made for them. They were homeless and separated from the Lord. This was the byproduct of listening to the wrong voice, the voice of ungodly counsel.

Poor Counsel Produces Poor Decisions

Listening to wrong voices will cause poor decisions. We see this happening with Adam and Eve, and it is prevalent in the world today. Unfortunately, it is not an uncommon problem in the Church. Christians listen to unwise counsel and do foolish things while doing it in the name of the Lord. Wrong voices and bad counsel lead good people down the wrong path and they do incorrect things. Sometimes they will do bizarre things.

As I shared in the opening of the first book in this *Voices Trilogy*, when people do not properly discern the voices they hear, they do crazy things. I have watched sane people do some insane things, all in the name of the counsel they received. I've heard them say, "I asked my friend, and they told me to do this." Sometimes they say, "My co-worker shared with me an article she read, and I thought it was a good idea." I have even heard, "I read it on Facebook."

I'm not saying that their friend or co-worker are bad people. I'm sure they are well-meaning people who never want to lead someone astray. However, the counsel these friends gave was bad advice. It caused undesirable fruit and made a bad situation even worse. It poured fuel on a burning fire rather than quench the destructive blaze.

Anointed People Can Give Ungodly Counsel

People can even have an anointing on their lives and still give ungodly counsel. Let's look at examples of this in the Bible:

> Look, these women caused the children of Israel, through the counsel of Balaam, to trespass against the LORD in the incident of Peor, and there was a plague among the congregation of the LORD (Numbers 31:16).

> Then said Absalom to Ahithophel, Give counsel among you what we shall do. And Ahithophel said unto Absalom, Go in unto thy father's concubines, which he hath left to keep the house; and all Israel shall hear that thou art abhorred of thy father: then shall the hands of all that are with thee be strong. So they spread Absalom a tent upon the top of the house; and Absalom went in unto his father's concubines in the sight of all Israel. And the counsel of Ahithophel, which he counselled in those days, was as if a man had inquired at the oracle of God: so was all the counsel of Ahithophel both with David and with Absalom (2 Samuel 16:20-23, KJV).

There are two different men that we read about in the above passages of Scripture: Balaam and Ahithophel. Both men had God-given prophetic giftings; however, both gave wrong counsel that resulted in negative consequences for those who listened. They were anointed of the Lord yet yielded their voices to speak wrongly to those they were to lead in the paths of righteousness.

It is important to understand that words coming out of someone's mouth posed as counsel does not guarantee their accuracy. The anointing that rests upon someone's life does not alone ensure that their counsel is unadulterated and solid. Good people can give bad counsel. Their voice can be tainted, resulting in wrong direction and instruction. Sometimes, the result in the lives of those who listen to and heed their bad counsel can be disastrous.

On several occasions throughout my life and ministry, I observed Christians receiving bad counsel from someone they believed cared for them and would speak the truth. However, the counsel they received was inaccurate, leading to devastating situations. I have seen relationships destroyed because of wrong counsel given and then heeded. I have seen families wrecked because of the same. Bad advice has led many good people down the wrong road.

The individuals giving the inaccurate counsel were not bad people. However, their inability to correctly discern the situation, along with their predisposition and ignorance, caused their well-meaning advice to turn into destructive directives. These God-loving people turned into the mouthpiece of the enemy.

So Glad I Didn't Listen

When I was much younger, I had the opportunity to discuss some matters concerning family relationships and priorities with an admired and anointed man of God. I respected him greatly, and he was a tremendous teacher of the Word. He possessed some wonderful revelation and illumination of the Bible.

During our meeting, he looked at me and said, "You should not prioritize your spouse and family over your ministry call. The priority of your relationship with God and ministry cannot be separated; they are one and the same." When he said it, I immediately had bells and alarms going off inside of me. I knew his counsel at that moment was bad because it was unbiblical and skewed.

Fortunately, I discerned this quickly because of my knowledge of the Word and the witness of the Holy Spirit. I recognized that He was speaking out of his opinion on this matter, as evidenced in his own family. He possessed an incorrect interpretation of Scripture in this area.

I knew that God created the home before He created ministry and the Church. The top priority that anyone has after their personal relationship with the Lord is their relationship with their spouse. The apostle Paul said that if a man cannot rule his own family well, it disqualifies him from ministry in the house of the Lord. That truth by itself reveals family has priority over ministry.

Years later, this anointed man of God had marital problems and divorced his wife. He later remarried and then divorced again. Contrastingly, my wife and I have been married for over 40 years and have been in ministry for the same. We also have three wonderful children and nine grandchildren who serve God today.

I did not share this story to condemn a man of God but rather to reveal how his counsel bore bad fruit in his own life and would have also borne the same in my life if I heeded it. I am so glad that I did not listen to his counsel. Even though he was mightily anointed, flowed in the gifts of the Spirit, and taught the Word of God with power and gifting, his counsel to me at that moment was misguided.

Good People and Ungodly Counsel

It is imperative for us to understand that a well-meaning, good-hearted person can give ungodly counsel. This does not mean they are backslidden or unholy; it simply means that their good intentions did not translate into good counsel. They rendered advice that was incorrect for the individual they sought to help. There can be numerous reasons for this dynamic taking place. Some of them have already been discussed in previous chapters of this book.

A blessing is released within the lives of those who refuse to walk in ungodly counsel. The Psalmist said they would be like a tree planted by rivers of living water. He went on to say they would be fruitful, and their leaf would not wither. These blessings occur in the lives of people who refuse to listen to wrong counsel yet will embrace godly directives. As a result, their lives are filled with the blessing of the Lord, and good things happen to them.

This is a simple principle: Those who listen to and heed good counsel will experience good things; those who listen to and heed bad counsel will experience bad things. Embracing the good produces what is good, and embracing the bad produces what is bad. It is just that simple.

Good Intentions Do Not Determine Good Counsel

Someone can have a heart of gold and still give bad counsel. Many people are led astray with their best friend whispering in their ear. While their intentions may be good, their counsel can be bad. I have seen it happen on more than one occasion.

An individual came into my office for counsel regarding marital problems. As we discussed their issues, they shared that they planned to separate from their spouse. When I asked them why they would do such a thing, they said, "I talked to my friend, and they told me to do it." When I asked about the person giving bad advice, I was informed they had been divorced numerous times and currently were separated from their spouse.

Think about this for a moment. A lifelong decision is augmented by a friend speaking unbiblical counsel. Instead of coming to their pastor first, they sought advice from a friend. The individual giving the wrong counsel had no business offering any advice at the time. They were not in a position and failed to possess a proper platform to counsel anyone concerning marriage.

Regardless of how much you endear someone, it does not equate with them speaking sound advice. These loved ones can even speak in tongues and prophesy yet still give unbiblical counsel. Love for an individual cannot be the determining factor for listening to their voice. Things said by anyone must be weighed and measured by the standard of God's Word. If it fails to measure up, then tell it to shut up!

I recognize those are strong words. However, accurate and godly counsel for your life and family is more important than feelings. I had to do this with bad counsel given to me by a leader in the Church when I was much younger. While I did not verbally tell them to shut up, I said internally, "I rebuke you." I recognized that their counsel did not measure up to the standard of the Word of God.

Ishmaels Produced by Bad Counsel

Now Sarai Abram's wife bare him no children: and she had an handmaid, an Egyptian, whose name was Hagar. And Sarai said unto Abram, Behold now, the LORD hath restrained me from bearing: I pray thee, go in unto my maid; it may be that I may obtain children by her. And Abram hearkened to the voice of Sarai. And Sarai Abram's wife took Hagar her maid the Egyptian, after Abram had dwelt ten years in the land of Canaan, and gave her to her husband Abram to be his wife. And he went in unto Hagar, and she conceived: and when she saw that she had conceived, her mistress was despised in her eyes. And Sarai said unto Abram, My wrong be upon thee: I have given

my maid into thy bosom; and when she saw
that she had conceived, I was despised in her
eyes: the LORD judge between me and thee
(Genesis 16:1-5, KJV).

Sarai became frustrated that she was not pregnant. The
fulfillment of God's promise was not happening according to
her timetable. Thus, she decided to take matters into her own
hands by setting up her maid, Hagar, to have a sexual encounter
with her husband, Abram. There is no indication that he
objected or argued with Sarai at all. Abram was ready, willing,
and able to oblige his wife's counsel. Once the ordeal was
completed, and Hagar conceived, Sarai became angry and
bitter. Unfortunately, it was too late.

Abraham listened to the voice of a friend; he heeded wrong
counsel spoken by his wife, Sarah. By doing so, he made a
mistake. Listening to poor counsel produced Ishmael.
Abraham created an issue rather than an heir. Listening to
ungodly counsel will produce undesirable things in a person's
life.

It is reasonable to say that Sarah's intentions were good. She
felt as though she was holding up the fulfillment of God's
promise and wanted to help speed things up. It is very possible
that she felt like a failure in her inability to give Abraham a
child. I am sure that despair attacked her mind. All these things
combined to produce a fleshly plan in Sarah's mind that
bypassed God's work.

Abraham's fault was found in heeding Sarah's counsel. His
transgression was realized by listening to the voice of his friend.
Even Sarah said that the wrong was found in Abraham heeding

her counsel. **Here is a valuable lesson, the greater wrong is found in heeding ungodly counsel, even more so than giving it.** We are responsible for the decisions we make regardless of the voices that we hear. We are responsible for determining what is right and what is wrong.

Can't Point the Finger

We must understand that we can never point our finger at someone else and blame them for the bad counsel we heed. We are responsible for discerning what we hear. Eve attempted to blame the serpent in the Garden of Eden. However, she was still held accountable for mistaking the deceiver's voice for the voice of a friend and counselor. God does not give us the right to excuse ourselves from the responsibility of heeding ungodly counsel. We are held accountable for the decisions we make.

Sarah said Abraham's wrong was found in heeding her voice. Her counsel was given to him in a time of despair and desperation. Abraham should have discerned this and refused to be swayed by the words of his wife. Instead, he willingly submitted to her suggestion and made a horrible decision. If Abraham had refused to listen to Sarah, all the resulting consequences would have been avoided. His failure to say "no" to the counsel of his wife brought undesired fruit.

I am quite sure that Sarah's intentions were well-meaning; she wanted to ensure that Abraham had children. She believed she could do something to assist in the situation. However, good intentions never make counsel correct or godly.

Be Careful the Company You Keep

Many Christians corrupt themselves by keeping the wrong company. Their relationship pool is tainted by maintaining close companionship with less than savory people. They fellowship regularly with those who are worldly in their speech and behavior. This friendship can negatively impact the lives of believers because of the ungodly influence that it imposes.

> "Be not deceived: evil communications corrupt good manners" (1 Corinthians 15:33, KJV).

Paul made sure the believers at Corinth understood that they were not to keep close company with those who were unsaved and godless. The word "communications" literally means *companionship*. In other words, maintaining ungodly companions and friends will corrupt you. The speech and behavior of those who live in a worldly manner will contaminate the life of a believer. This is what Paul said.

We are tasked with the responsibility of witnessing to the lost. However, we are warned against having close intimate relationships with unbelievers. We are also encouraged to avoid those who call themselves Christians yet engage in a sinful lifestyle. Getting close to these kinds of people will corrupt the good within believers.

How often have you heard parents say to their children, "Don't be hanging out with those kids!" When our children were growing up, we instructed them to refrain from establishing relationships with certain people. It was not because we hated the other kids. We initiated these limitations because we loved our children and recognized these other kids could potentially contaminate and pollute our children. As a father, I was not punishing my children by forbidding relationships with other kids; my responsibility was to raise and train my children in the nurture and admonition of the Lord. These other kids posed a threat to my children being raised in that manner. Therefore, I restricted them from having close friendships with kids that demonstrated poor attitudes and behavior.

Anyone who hangs around a sinner will end up sinning. Those who develop a close companionship with a drunkard will end up drinking themselves. If you hang around negative people, you will become negative. We become the company we keep because our lives are influenced by the voices and behavior we experience around us. Therefore, we must always be cautious about who we befriend in a close manner.

While not every friend gives bad counsel, friendship does not guarantee it to be godly and right. The test for accurate voices must be given for everything that we hear. Failure to do so can cause catastrophic consequences.

It Must Pass the Test

Here are a few questions you can ask to test the voices that you hear. If it fails the test, you are responsible to reject the voice, even if it comes from the person you most admire. Therefore, we must pose these test questions to the voices we hear:

- Is it in agreement with God's Word?
- Does it articulate the heart and spirit of Jesus?

- Does it provoke one to godly or ungodly behavior?
- Does it provoke one to love people or hate people?
- Does it confront improper attitudes, or does it justify them?
- Does it vilify others, or does it exhibit longsuffering?
- Does it legitimize hatred for others, or does it convict the heart for ill will toward others?
- Does it justify sinful conduct, or does it admonish to avoid it?

If any question cannot be answered with a correct biblical response, then the voice should be discarded and rejected. If you desire the blessing of the Lord to be manifested within your life, you must refuse to walk in ungodly counsel.

The blessed man does not heed wrong voices; he discards them from his life. The blessed man does not listen to unbiblical counsel; he refuses to receive it. The blessed man does not hear the voice of the ungodly; he boldly rejects it.

Ask the Lord to help you discard wrong voices so you can walk in His blessing. Ask the Holy Spirit for spiritual enlightenment to show you what is good or bad. Doing this is the pathway to the blessing of the Lord. The blessed man does not walk in the counsel of the ungodly; he rejects the voices of deception.

VOICES 2

9

ROBBED BY DOUBT

> Now the serpent was more cunning than any
> beast of the field which the LORD God had
> made. And he said to the woman, "Has God
> indeed said, 'You shall not eat of every tree of
> the garden'?" (Genesis 3:1).

The voice of doubt is one that robs many believers from receiving the full blessing God desires for their lives. It prevents people from entering the fulfillment of God's promise and redemptive realities. It is the voice that questions what God has said. Doubt is at the root of the fall of man. It is at the foundation of a shipwrecked life that needs rescuing.

Going back to the account of Adam and Eve in the Garden of Eden, the first thing that comes specifically out of the mouth of the serpent is, "Has God indeed said?" The attempt to deceive began with questioning what God had spoken. The serpent questioned not only what God had said but also His motives for what He commanded both Adam and Eve. When they entertained the question posed by the serpent, they sank quickly.

Questioning what God said is the voice of doubt. Once the bait is taken, it opens the door for the thief and the robber to come. When questions concerning the validity of what God said enter a person's mind, they must combat them with the voice of truth. The voice of doubt seems to always end with a question mark. Contrastingly, the voice of truth ends with an exclamation point.

Doubt Robs Inheritance

The first manifestation of the enemy's voice within the earth was seeds of doubt and unbelief. This started Eve on a journey that did not end well for her and Adam. The door of doubt sent her down a road that led to deception and destruction.

If the devil can get you to doubt what God said, he will rob you of your inheritance. Adam and Eve were banished from the Garden of Eden; they lost everything they knew to be their home. The very place created to be inhabited by them became desolate because they were removed from the garden, so it no longer had caretakers. Ultimately, the beautiful garden that God planted became barren. The inheritance that Adam and Eve were given was lost because they listened to the voice of doubt.

Some believers today forfeit their inheritance because they allow a place for doubt in their hearts and minds. The voice of doubt is the sound that is only asking questions. It will manipulate the voice of human reasoning to question the validity of the Lord's proclamations.

Unfortunately, believers trade their birthright for the package the voice of doubt holds. When they open the box, they only find a picture of what they forfeited which will never be experienced. They exchange their promise for the package named doubt. Their inheritance is traded for the box of questions that the voice of doubt delivered.

Doubt Is Believing the Wrong Voice

It is essential to understand that operating in doubt does not mean one no longer believes. Much of our thought process has associated doubt with failure to believe; however, doubting merely believes the wrong voice. To doubt means that someone is believing the voice of doubt—the voice of the enemy. Doubt results from making an incorrect choice of what voice to believe.

When the voice of doubt speaks, it will often disguise itself as the truth seeker. This is what the serpent did with Eve. He said that the moment Eve ate of the tree, she would be enlightened and be like God. So, the pathway to doubting what God said was paved with the false promise of enlightenment. Doubt was disguised as the revealer of truth.

Just as satan does not announce his arrival, neither does the voice of doubt. It will not say, *"I am doubt, and I've come to steal your promise."* Instead, it declares that it is the conveyer of truth and revelation. It will shout that it has come to show forth the more perfect way of the Lord. This is precisely what the serpent did with Eve.

Doubt is the language of hell; it is not heaven's language. It is the voice that seeks to steal, kill, and destroy. Failure to discern it will end in an invasion of hell within one's life. Its mission is to restrain believers from receiving the fullness of their inheritance and promise. It will dishearten, discourage, and distress anyone who falls prey to its lies.

If the enemy cannot keep someone from getting saved, he will then focus on keeping them from their inheritance. He does this because believers pose no threat to his kingdom when they forfeit their purpose and destiny. When they trade in their birthright at the bidding of the voice of doubt, the enemy can invade, maraud, and embezzle the future God has for them. Therefore, we must say "no" when doubt rears its head. Crush it beneath your feet by refusing to give it place in your life.

Give No Place to the Devil

Paul specifically commanded believers to give no place to the devil (Ephesians 4:27). We must not allow a place in our minds to be open to the voice of doubt. If we fill our minds and hearts with the Word of God, there will be no room for doubt to take up residency. It is simple; if the space is occupied by the truth of God's Word, there is no room for anything else.

The Passion Translation translates this verse like this:

"Don't give the slanderous accuser, the Devil, an opportunity to manipulate you!" (Ephesians 4:27, TPT).

Many believers give the devil opportunities to manipulate them into believing things, saying things, and doing things contrary to Scripture. Most of the time, they fail to realize they are being controlled by satan. They become like a marionette controlled by a puppet master. The entire time they believe they are following God's will for their lives while oblivious to who is pulling the strings.

Good People Manipulated by a Bad Devil

As a pastor, I have seen this happen far too many times. Good people were controlled by a bad devil because they gave place in their lives to the voice of doubt and unbelief. They gave the enemy opportunity through an open door. They were not filled with the Word, so the empty spot in their lives created a vacuum that the enemy was obliged to fill. They were manipulated into yielding to the voice of doubt, forfeiting their promise, and leaving the place of blessing with a souvenir piece of clothing, just like Adam and Eve.

This kind of thing happens needlessly for Christians. It is all because the wrong voice is pulling the strings in their lives. The enemy takes advantage of a place within them that can be manipulated by the voice of doubt, fear, unbelief, and skepticism.

This is what took place within Adam and Eve; they gave place to the voice of doubt. The fact that they entertained the voice of the serpent reveals there was a place in their minds and hearts that was not filled properly with the things of God. There was an area void of what was needed that only the Lord could fill. As a result, the enemy's voice found a place by which he could manipulate them into sinning against God.

Again, the solution to this issue is for one to be filled with the Word of God and the Spirit of the Lord. When we are filled with Him, there is no place or opportunity for the voice of the enemy to control or manipulate us. Fill yourself with the Lord, His presence, His Word, and His Spirit. If the enemy can find no place in you, he will leave and go elsewhere. Send the devil packing by being filled up with the good things of God.

> Now in the fourth watch of the night Jesus went to them, walking on the sea. And when the disciples saw Him walking on the sea, they were troubled, saying, "It is a ghost!" And they cried out for fear. But immediately Jesus spoke to them, saying, "Be of good cheer! It is I; do not be afraid." And Peter answered Him and said, "Lord, if it is You, command me to come to You on the water." So He said, "Come." And when Peter had come down out of the boat, he walked on the water to go to Jesus. But when he saw that the wind was boisterous, he was afraid; and beginning to sink he cried out, saying, "Lord, save me!" And immediately Jesus stretched out His hand and caught him, and said to him, "O you of little faith, why did you doubt?" (Matthew 14:25-31).

This passage of Scripture is familiar to most Christians. I recall hearing this story as a little boy in Sunday School and Children's Church. It was exciting to hear about Jesus walking on water.

The account of Peter walking on water and then sinking has been preached from pulpits by ministers across the world, with varying truths brought to light. I have heard numerous messages preached from this wonderful passage of Scripture. However, I want to approach this from a different perspective in this writing.

When we speak of doubt, we recognize that at the base level, doubt is disbelieving something that has been said to us. We choose to believe something different. The reasons we doubt can be varied. However, most of the time, it is based upon our experience with the person that spoke something to us or a previous experience in a similar situation or circumstance. Our life experiences create a baseline of what we believe and what we doubt.

For instance, someone promised to do something a year ago and never did it after repeated promises of completion. Afterward, they return and tell us they will get it done immediately. Typically, we do not believe them because their history declares they will not perform what they say they will do. Our experience with them promotes that we doubt what they say.

Peter's Experience

After walking with Jesus for years, Peter was assured that Jesus would do what He said. So, Peter's doubt was rooted in something other than disbelief in the words of Jesus. I propose his doubt was rooted in his personal experience with the sea as a professional fisherman.

For close to 30 years, Peter was a fisherman before becoming Jesus' disciple. He had tremendous knowledge of the sea, and I am sure he had personal knowledge of people drowning in similar stormy situations. It is possible that he knew of people fishing in poor conditions who never returned. Peter had tremendous experience on the water and maintained a healthy respect for the sea.

Doubt came to life when his experience shouted louder than the words Jesus spoke. He believed the voice of his previous professional experience. Peter saw and felt the wind, and it spoke to him. The voice of his experience empowered the voice of doubt. His experience told him, "*People die in these conditions.*" His experience told him, "*Waves like this cause boats to capsize and people to drown.*" His experience told him, "*I should be at home with mama and the kids, not out here in the middle of a storm.*"

The voice of doubt usually seems reasonable. All of Peter's experiences were correct and true. Peter's knowledge and understanding of the sea were not that of a landlubber. He had intimate knowledge of boat capabilities, sea conditions, and storm dangers. These things were all true and accurate, but they resulted in him sinking and needing to be rescued. The voice of doubt took control of Peter's mind and heart.

A legitimate truthful fact can become the megaphone for the voice of doubt. Experience has the potential to empower doubt's voice to scream in your ear. The only way to silence the voice of doubt is to increase the volume of the promises God has spoken. The voice of the Lord must become louder and carry greater weight than contrary voices that seek to crowd the mind.

Overcoming Your Experience

In my first book on voices, I share the testimony of the miraculous birth of our daughter. After my wife conceived, she began to bleed heavily. The official diagnosis was that she had a blighted ovum. The doctor instructed my wife to have a D&C procedure since the embryo had died. However, we had accurate prophetic words that contradicted the voice of medical science. So, we decided to stand upon God's promise.

During this time, the voice of doubt was attempting to crowd our minds. Years previously, my wife, Stacey, experienced a miscarriage and had a D&C procedure because there was no embryo in her uterus. This previous experience was screaming in our ears that this was the same thing happening again. The voice of our previous experience was the enemy of our faith. It was empowering the voice of doubt to be heard in our ears.

Along with this, Stacey was experiencing symptoms daily. She had to see blood every time she went to the bathroom and was constantly bombarded by her senses that contradicted the prophetic promise given to us. Empowered by experience, the voice of doubt continually screamed in her ear.

The Promise Must Become Louder

I remember us rehearsing the prophetic promises that were declared over us daily. We took those words and warred with them. We made declarations through prayer as I would lay my hands on Stacey's stomach and say, "You will live and not die!" Our declaration had to become louder than the voice of doubt, and it did!

Ultimately, we saw God move, and all the bleeding stopped. About two months after the initial diagnosis, Stacey returned to the doctor, and they placed a fetal heart monitor on her stomach. Much to the doctor's surprise, they immediately heard a strong heartbeat. Hallelujah, the voice of doubt was defeated, and the voice of the Lord had won! On December 6, 1988, Stacey gave birth to our daughter, Kayla.

I want to point out that the original doctor's diagnosis was not incorrect. However, it contradicted a valid prophetic declaration made over our lives. Our previous experience was true and authentic. However, we could not give it weight since it was contrary to God's promise, and it would enable the voice of doubt. Therefore, we had to say, "Let God be true, and every man a liar!"

It Ain't Easy

When you are walking through difficult and adverse situations, it is not easy. At times, it can be quite difficult and trying. The voice of doubt will shout to you as legitimate experiences empower it. You will hear, *"This will be just like it was last time."* The devil will attempt to take advantage of your yesterday to defraud you of your promised tomorrow. His goal is to rob you of the fulfillment of God's destiny and purpose for your life. It is the same thing he did in the Garden with Eve. The voice of doubt led her down a path of deception that ended with the forfeiture of her inheritance.

The voice of doubt has one desired outcome, and that is to bankrupt your promise. It wants you to write a check that hands over your promise: spiritually, physically, financially, and familially. Its goal is to rob, kill, and destroy through the introduction of questioning the very thing that God has spoken.

The Key to Overcoming

The key to overcoming this hideous voice is to elevate the proper voices. The voice of doubt is silenced when the voice of the Lord rings louder. God's voice rings louder through speaking it out with your own mouth.

Jesus silenced the voice of doubt and deception when He was tempted by speaking God's written Word. In every situation, Jesus said, "It is written!" Jesus knew the written Word and, therefore, was able to wield it as a sword to silence contrary voices. Unfortunately, many believers today have little knowledge of the written Word and fall prey to the voices of doubt and deception because of their ignorance. Others become victims because of their lack of persistence and endurance.

It is imperative to understand that fighting doubt can be a fight for life and death. The struggle can be difficult. However, if we renew our minds to God's promise, meditate on His Word, and make declarations of faith, we will silence the voice of doubt and arise in victory. Hallelujah!

Contrary to Biblical Truth

The voice of doubt and unbelief possesses a recognizable language. It speaks that which is contrary to established biblical truth. It speaks in a language that contradicts the teaching ministry, demonstrative ministry, and redemptive ministry of

Jesus. The language of doubt possesses no truth because satan is the author of it; he wrote and composed it himself.

Jesus said that satan is a liar. He went on to say that there is no truth in anything the devil says. You know the devil is lying because his lips are moving; it is impossible for him to speak the truth.

When believers are knowledgeable of the Word of God, it becomes easy for them to discern the voice of doubt and unbelief. When a Christian renews their mind, they can sense when doubt and unbelief are given voice. Spiritual alarms begin to be set off inside them when things are biblically untrue, which is the byproduct of believers having their spiritual senses exercised to discern good and evil. Those who handle the truth through study, prayer, and meditation of the Word will overcome this dangerous voice and avoid its pitfalls.

> For everyone who partakes only of milk is
> unskilled in the word of righteousness, for he is
> a babe. But solid food belongs to those who are
> of full age, that is, those who by reason of use
> have their senses exercised to discern both good
> and evil (Hebrews 5:13-14).

The writer of Hebrews said that our spiritual senses can be exercised. This action is the key to accurate spiritual discernment. Our senses are exercised as we spend time in prayer and digest God's Word daily. By doing so, we tune our spirit man to the channel from where God is broadcasting. Hearing what God is speaking causes an immediate rejection of false information from the enemy, which disables the voice of doubt and unbelief.

In the context of this Scripture, exercising your spiritual senses and discernment have a direct correlation to one's skill level in God's Word. Those who have moved on from the milk of the Word and have grown to eat and digest the meat are the ones who can discern what is good from what is evil.

Know the Word

Over the years of my personal experience, I have found that those who have little working Bible knowledge equally have weak spiritual discernment. Proper spiritual discernment is directly linked to being skilled in the Word of God. Developing this skill requires time, study, and dedication. Unfortunately, these are qualities that are scarce among most Christians today.

We live in an "add water and stir" culture. We want things quick, and we desire them to require no work on our part. The cultural trend is to look for shortcuts to everything. The YouTube® generation has discovered the Oasis of Wisdom to be found in videos they can download from the internet. Study and dedication seem to be a fad of the past. Unfortunately, this has caused the church pulpits to become decreasingly theological and increasingly entertainment-based. All of this has resulted in producing a Church that possesses little discernment because they are biblically ignorant.

The only way that the level of discernment will increase within the body of Christ is through spiritual growth in biblical understanding. Attending another seminar on the gifts of the Spirit, although a good thing, will not by itself increase one's ability to discern. If someone is biblically ignorant before attending the seminar, chances are they will still lack needed knowledge after it is completed.

I am not saying that seminars and conferences are not useful. However, it will never replace someone's personal time of study, meditation, and prayer. Six hours of teaching at a seminar will not make up for six years of never opening one's Bible. Maturity is not attained overnight; it requires time and dedication.

Dedication Is Required

We recognize in most every other area of life that commitment and dedication are required for success. For example, anyone desiring to excel in an area of sports cannot attend a three-day football camp and become Tom Brady on day four. Becoming a good football player requires multiple years of hard work. This is true in all sports activities.

I played the trumpet when I was younger, starting in the 7th grade. I practiced daily and worked hard at becoming skillful. I also took lessons to learn to play the piano. By the time I was in the 9th grade, I was arranging music for the Jazz Band. When I was in 10th grade, I was composing wind instrument parts to accompany the youth choir in our church. I started directing and arranging music for our youth choir when I was sixteen. By the time I was seventeen, I was writing music and directing the adult choir.

When I started playing the trumpet in 7th grade, I sounded like a cow bellowing in a pasture. However, by the time I was in college, I was an accomplished player, the principal trumpet in the college orchestra, and improv soloist in the Jazz Band.

I do not share any of my accomplishments to beat myself on the chest. I share this to point out the fact that this did not happen because an angel of the Lord came into my room at midnight and touched my hands, resulting in a miraculous musical impartation. It happened because I worked and dedicated myself to developing those skills. I lived in a practice room and spent a minimum of four hours daily working on these things.

The unfortunate thing today is that believers want to walk through a "prayer tunnel" to receive an impartation of discernment abilities but are not willing to open their Bibles at night because they don't want to miss the latest Netflix® series. Many want the "add water and stir" method that does not exist. If you want to possess keen discernment, you must become a student of the Word, and this is the road that will cause your spiritual senses to be exercised.

The Balance

I want to add some balance to some of the things I've shared in this chapter to ensure these truths are not taken out of context or to an extreme. Any truth taken to an extreme can cause people to be harmed due to inappropriate application.

We must understand that unless we have a specific promise in the Bible or a proven prophetic Word on a matter, we should not ignore experience or what we see. So, walking in faith is not synonymous with ignoring everything we see. We live in a natural world that gives us information from which we make logical decisions. This is a good thing because God created things in this manner.

I do not have a word from the Lord nor a promise that allows me to walk on water like Peter. Jesus was present with Peter and told him to get out of the boat and come to Him. I have never seen Jesus walk on water, nor has He ever told me to step out of the boat to walk with Him. Therefore, I will stay in the boat when I am sailing.

I own a small boat suitable for taking out in the bay or ocean, provided the seas are not greater than three to four feet. While it may handle some larger seas, it is not wise to take it out in those conditions. My family considers me a safety nut. I never go out without ample life vests, flares, fuel, water, and a working horn to get someone's attention if I get in trouble. I check everything out on the boat inside and out before it is launched into the water. I do this because it is wisdom to do so and has nothing to do with doubting God's promise of protection. It is the realization that one can potentially forfeit their promise if they act out of stupidity.

Far too many believers do unwise things in the name of faith. Then when they have negative consequences for their actions, they blame God for not coming through for them. My friend, faith does not ignore conventional wisdom. Silencing the voice of doubt does not mean we should act unwisely.

Medical Science and Doubt

Similarly, the use of medical science does not mean that you are heeding the voice of doubt. Jesus traveled with a doctor (likely practicing holistic medicine). He even said, "They that be whole need not a physician, but they that are sick" (Matthew 9:12, KJV). Jesus never discouraged the practice of medical science, nor did He give any indication that the use of it signified doubt.

In recent years, some Christians have taken an anti-medical science position. For various reasons, they have demonized different medical breakthroughs and even called some of them the "mark of the beast." My friend, the mark of the beast spoken of in the book of Revelation has absolutely nothing to do with medical science or any medical breakthrough.

Christians must stop with these types of shenanigans. This misapplication of Scripture and misinformation does great harm to the body of Christ and the people that believe these erroneous declarations. We are never allowed to take a verse of Scripture out of context and use it to justify our disapproval of something based solely upon our opinion or preferences. God's Word was never intended to be manipulated to impose and propagate opinions on which the Bible is silent.

I believe God for protection and have no doubt that His angels are encamped around me. However, I still put on my seatbelt in an automobile. I also lock my doors at night when I am sleeping in my house. There are those that I know who possess firearms for the purpose of personal protection. So, does possessing a firearm equate to listening to the voice of doubt? I do not believe that it does. Owning a firearm does not mean you are doubting or questioning God's promise of protection.

Using natural wisdom and common sense is not equivalent to listening to the voice of doubt. It is only when things labeled as common sense contradict God's spoken promise that it can become doubt. It is important to properly discern the use of natural wisdom contrasted with listening to the voice of doubt.

Disabling Doubt

The voice of doubt has robbed many Christians of their inheritance. The same tactics satan used in the Garden of Eden, he still uses today. There is not a new technique that the enemy is using. It is the same song being sung with a new audience to listen to it. The devil has no new tricks up his sleeve just now being revealed. He continues to cause people to stumble with the same old mechanisms.

Adam and Eve forfeited their home and everything they were given because they gave place to the voice of doubt. Peter sank after walking on water because of doubt. The list of people could continue both in the Bible and those I personally know who handed over their inheritance because of listening to the voice of doubt.

We must disable and silence this deadly voice, and we do it by amplifying the voice of the Lord and His Word. It is done through continual meditation and consecration to the Lord. It is accomplished by the renewing of our minds and keen spiritual discernment. These are the ways that we disable the voice of doubt.

We must rise in the power of the Holy Spirit and silence this voice within our lives. We must say, *"Let God be true, and every man a liar."* We choose to believe every promise of God and disable the voice of the enemy. Doubt will have no dominion in my life. God's Word is the final authority and my final answer.

Pray this with me today:

Father, I choose to believe your Word. Your promises are "yes" and "amen" to my family and me. Doubt will have no place in my life because I choose to fortify myself with your Word. My mind is daily renewed as I meditate and confess Your promises. The voice of doubt is silenced as the declarations of heaven ring loud in my heart and my hearing. In Jesus' name, I pray, Amen!

VOICES 2

10

PROPHETIC NONSENSE

"But he who prophesies speaks edification and exhortation and comfort to men" (1 Corinthians 14:3).

In my book *Voices—Hearing and Discerning When God Speaks,* I write in-depth on the value of the prophetic ministry. God has placed the gift of prophecy in the Church for the purpose of building up and encouraging the body of Christ. Therefore, the ministry gift of the prophet should be embraced by every Christian. These gifts that God has purposed within the Church are needed for the maturity of believers so they can then do the work of the ministry. Failure to embrace the prophetic ministry in its biblical entirety will lead to spiritually weak and frail believers.

In my previous book, I give numerous examples and testimonies of the importance of prophets in today's Church. There are so many wonderful things that I have personally experienced because of the prophetic ministry. I cannot overstate the value and need for prophets, the gift of prophecy, and prophetic people to be activated in their gifts and callings.

With that said, it is equally important for us to identify anything which may be false or misleading that is branded as prophetic. The way to determine the counterfeit is by handling the real; handling the authentic and accurate will cause what is false to become apparent. We have the responsibility to identify what is misleading so that gullible believers will not fall prey to it. Doing this also prevents things that are not genuine from being fostered and reproduced within the Church.

The Prophetic and Current Events

The entire world suffered a pandemic, and the United States held its 2020 presidential election at the writing of this book. Great debate and disagreement surrounded all of these national and international events. Numerous things were prophesied concerning these national challenges and obstacles. Many prophecies were given concerning the COVID virus along with specific dates or seasons for its end. There were also prophetic words concerning the U.S. election. Additionally, there were other prophecies about different situations occurring in our nation and the world that sometimes seemed to contradict one another.

We realize most of these prognostications failed to materialize, leaving many searching for answers as to why and how these things could be. Much of this received national attention from secular media outlets resulting in stories and articles that were less than flattering toward prophets and prophetic ministers. Within the prophetic ministry at large, this created a call for purity and integrity. I believe God is calling for an introspective look.

Clean Up Is Not Persecution

It is essential to understand that confrontation of what is error should not be labeled as persecution. When God begins to call for the Church to clean up the mess, we cannot be upset about it. When a grocery store announces, "*Clean up on aisle 6*," it is not to harm the working employees but to protect their customers. So likewise, the Holy Spirit is calling for an honest evaluation of things being done in the name of the prophetic ministry so the Church will be protected.

The tendency of human behavior is to ignore and cover up things that create issues and problems. In relation to the prophetic ministry, I believe this is not the correct course of action. While many prophets and prophetic ministers recently spoke presumptuously and unwisely about numerous things, we must realize that most did not. It is important for us to avoid making rash decisions based on the behavior of those who handled things incorrectly. We should not throw the baby out with the bath water; clean the baby and discard the dirty water.

I believe that many prophetic ministers who made false or presumptuous prophetic declarations possess a heart to bless the Church. From most of these, I never sensed any ill intent. While some motives could be questioned, the majority had a desire to build and encourage the body of Christ.

As was said earlier in this writing, intentions alone do not make a word correct or accurate. A person can have the intention to bless someone yet still prophesy inaccurately. A prophet can love the Lord yet allow his heart to become crowded with theories and falsehoods that negatively affect the word they deliver. Ministers and believers can possess the greatest intentions and be the nicest people but totally mistake an illegitimate voice for the voice of the Lord. These things happened historically and still happen today.

Prophetic Nonsense

I have been a Christian my entire life and have been actively involved in ministry for over 40 years. I have seen a lot come and go throughout my life. There have been different spiritual waves that have crashed on the shores of the Church during various seasons. Most of it has been good and brought the Church to a greater understanding and demonstration of the purpose of God. However, there have been some things that revealed the weakness and inability of the Church to discern properly. I refer to some of these things taking place as prophetic nonsense.

I call it prophetic nonsense because it was labeled as prophetic but was nothing more than nonsense. These things were unbiblical and brought confusion into the body of Christ because they were bizarre and could not be found in the Bible. The biblical precedent for these peculiarities did not exist anywhere in the Old or New Testaments. They lacked the ability to stand up against any biblical scrutiny.

There are some things that I have already specified in this writing which fall into this classification. I will not mention them again as you can reflect on what you have already read. However, there are a few that people have recently practiced that should be noted.

Denial Is Not Prophetic

There are some prophets and ministers who denied the very existence of the COVID virus. They posted videos and blogs saying that the Lord revealed to them it was not a real virus. In the meanwhile, hundreds of thousands of people died from COVID pneumonia. That is a fact, not fiction.

I had doctors and nurses in our church body who were daily tending to these patients. They are what I refer to as "boots on the ground." They possessed a working knowledge of what was happening to people hospitalized with COVID; they saw it every day. It was something they contended with that exasperated them beyond measure.

Some people in our church body lost family members to this disease. Almost everyone knows of someone (many of them Christians) who died from COVID during the pandemic. Yet, while these things were happening, there were some ministers and prophets saying it was nothing at all. Not only were they insensitive, but they were also wrong.

Prophets who do such things operate in prophetic nonsense. The prophetic ministry does not deny the existence of the present reality. Prophets may declare what the future holds that is different from the present situation. However, the prophetic ministry does not deny present realities or pretend they fail to exist. To do so is antithetical to the very nature of the prophetic ministry being revelatory; it reveals rather than conceals.

Lying Is Not Prophetic

Another example of prophetic nonsense is what happened on the heels of our most recent presidential election of 2020. After the inauguration, some prophets and ministers said that Joe Biden was not the president. Regardless of facts, regardless that he was sworn in, regardless that it was televised for the entire world to see, they declared the Lord revealed to them that he was not the president. It appears that they are not cognizant of the United States Constitution while stating how much they relish it.

The candidates or a person's vote is not the issue to which I am referring. I am speaking specifically of those who prophesy in the name of the Lord and say things that are nonsense. I heard ministers and believers promote theories that former President Donald Trump was still the president, and the activities seen on television with the newly elected President Joe Biden were merely green-screened illusions. Some of these prophets simultaneously complained about the nation's direction and blamed Joe Biden for the things taking place.

It does not take a rocket scientist to see the inconsistencies of their statements. These things happened primarily with various fringe prophetic camps. This is prophetic nonsense.

Some ministers told Christians to cease praying for our new president because he was not the "real" president. These ministers missed the entire instruction of Scripture and the spirit of our command to pray for leaders. Paul said to pray for all those in authority. It does not matter if you believe they are legitimately seated or not. Whether you like them or not, voted for them or not, the command still holds true. If someone holds a place of authority, pray for them; that is the command. To say God revealed something to you that is contrary to a biblical command is prophetic nonsense. We must call it what it is!

Understand these things are not said in defense of any political leader. This is strictly a matter of biblical principle. The fact is, I do not agree with many politicians on numerous issues that are dear to my heart. However, the Bible does not change according to who occupies the White House or any other seat of power. **Truthfully, the leaders we disagree with are the ones that need the most prayer. Think about it!**

Prophetic Signs in Athletics

In recent years, I have witnessed ministers attempting to make something prophetic from the winners of athletic events, the numbers on a football player's jersey, the score of a football game, and the way someone threw a baseball. Yes, ladies and gentlemen, I personally have witnessed and heard these things declared by those who claim to be prophets.

One prophet said that the score of a college football championship game was a prophetic sign of who would be president. However, his prognostication did not happen because it was prophetic nonsense. Yet another demonstration of this craziness manifested when a Super Bowl interception was said to be prophetic and touted as a sign of a politician returning to power.

To even allude that God is speaking through an athletic event is ludicrous. This is prophetic nonsense. Even if you believe this will happen or if it does take place in the future, to declare these types of things are prophetic signs or spiritual revelations is erroneous.

Not long ago, Dr. Fauci, the Chief Medical Advisor, threw the first pitch on the opening day of Major League Baseball. When he threw the ball, it went wide and short of the plate. Some prophets said this was a sign from God that he was crooked. The truth is many Christians did not like Dr. Fauci and attempted to interpret something spiritual from what had no spiritual significance at all. This is prophetic nonsense, regardless of what anyone thinks or believes about Dr. Fauci.

Given the opportunity to throw a baseball, most pastors and prophets would not be on target with their pitch either. Their ability to throw a baseball has no relevance to their ministries. An attempt to bring any parallel by observing their athletic abilities is preposterous. I will say it once again: these types of things are prophetic nonsense.

Correct Interpretation Is Needed

Please understand that what I am saying has nothing to do with certain politicians or personalities. It has nothing to do with anyone's opinion concerning any leader, whether good or bad. Instead, it is the principle of the matter. People ascribe the name of the Lord to their interpretations and perspectives of natural happenings, but they are nothing more than personal biases being overlayed on contemporary events. This is not how the prophetic is designed to operate within the Church.

We should never attempt to interpret the outcomes of athletic events or a person's athletic ability as a means whereby God is communicating. Christians are to be led by the Spirit, not the result of athletic events. We possess the indwelling voice of the Holy Spirit and do not need to interpret athletic contest scores as a sign from the Lord. These sorts of things are prophetic nonsense.

I recently spoke with someone concerning prophecies, dreams, visions, and other supernatural manifestations. They told me that if a prophecy or dream was articulated in their church and did not come to pass, it was considered as taking place "in the spirit" without manifestation in the natural realm. Therefore, anything uttered prophetically was considered accurate regardless of its perceivable fulfillment. Any prophecy or dream was accurate if delivered by a Christian, even if it failed to materialize. This is the position this church took. I shook my head in disbelief.

Here is the problem with that perspective: no prophecy or supernatural manifestation can be evaluated because it can always be said that it came to pass "in the spirit." This line of theological thinking is erroneous; it is heretical. It gives way to great error and misleading in the body of Christ.

The Fruit of the Voice

Jesus said a tree is known by the fruit that it bears. We should know ministers by their fruit. Any voice should be measured by the fruit that it possesses. Yes, you should be a fruit inspector, especially when it comes to voices you allow to influence your life. If the fruit of an individual's life is bad, I would recommend that you refrain from listening to their voice. This is not a statement of condemnation toward the individual, but rather one to save you from the same bad fruit that they already demonstrate.

To see your future, you need to go no further than examine the lives and fruit of the voices influencing you. If there are people who influence your life that are bearing bad fruit, you will do the same if you continue down the same path. However, if the people influencing your life are bearing good fruit, you will likewise bear good fruit.

If we see bad fruit, we are biblically responsible for discarding the voice. When we see good fruit, it would be wise to give an ear and listen to what they say. If what someone is declaring is not working in their own lives, then the chances are it may not work at all. The proof is always in the fruit.

If I desire to learn how to improve my marriage, I will not seek counsel from someone who has been divorced five times and whose current relationship is rocky. That is not a word of condemnation concerning anyone's past, but rather what is best for my future. If I want to succeed in business, I will not listen to someone lecture on success principles who recently filed for bankruptcy. Again, there is no condemnation for someone having a past failure. However, they must prove themselves before those principles are embraced by others.

Bad Fruit of Leaders

Jesus spoke of the bad fruit of the religious leaders. Along with this, He said to beware the leaven of the Pharisees, instructing His disciples to stay clear of things taught by the Pharisees. His command to those tasked with preaching the gospel was to refrain from listening to voices that possessed bad fruit. Why would Jesus say that? It is because bad fruit would taint their ministry of preaching the Good News.

We must observe the fruit of those who preach, teach, and prophesy. We should also look at the fruit that their voice produces in the lives of others. There are some messages and narratives that people promote which produce bad fruit. When the things someone is saying motivates and entices wrong behavior, we must remove that voice from our lives. If what they are teaching is producing ungodly behavior, we must disallow that voice to gain entrance to our hearts. If there is bad fruit around them, refuse to listen and take heed!

It is important for believers to understand that everything which is labeled prophetic is not necessarily from the Lord. There are things people speak to which they ascribe the name of the Lord while God never spoke it at all. There are those who are "spooky spiritual" and gravitate toward sensational things that God never authored. These sorts of things happen in the body of Christ regularly, and it is prophetic nonsense that needs to be identified as such.

Paul charged the Church with the responsibility of testing and proving all prophetic revelations and insight. Failure to do so will cause people to be led astray. We must evaluate things that are declared to be the voice of the Lord. If they do not pass the test of biblical scrutiny, they must be discarded and labeled as the voice of prophetic nonsense.

Everything that glitters is not gold. Everything that glows is not godly. Everything that gleams is not good. Things that may spiritually tantalize our ears are not necessarily authored in heaven. We must activate our spirit man to discern between that which is good and evil. This is the way that we can then reject the prophetic nonsense.

Jesus said to be wise as a serpent and harmless as a dove. Therefore, I encourage you to do what Jesus commanded by allowing the wisdom of God to fill you and walking in the love of God.

VOICES 2

11

CONDEMNATION IS NOT GOD'S NATURE

For God did not send His Son into the world to condemn the world, but that the world through Him might be saved. "He who believes in Him is not condemned; but he who does not believe is condemned already, because he has not believed in the name of the only begotten Son of God. And this is the condemnation, that the light has come into the world, and men loved darkness rather than light, because their deeds were evil (John 3:17-19).

"Condemnation" literally means *to damn or punish.* Jesus clearly stated that He did not come to condemn the world. Let that sink in for a moment. He said that He did not come to damn or punish the ungodly sinners. Instead, Jesus came to redeem, restore, and be the remedy. He came to save the world. He came to deliver those who were bound by satan's power.

The voice of condemnation will declare guilt, judgment, and punishment without any opportunity for redemption, restoration, or remedy. It has one goal: to push man away from reconciliation with God and His purpose. The voice of condemnation to the unsaved causes them to be ashamed and hide from the presence of the Lord in the same manner that Adam and Eve hid in the garden. It causes the believer to feel unworthy and robbed of their confidence in God. This voice seeks to separate man from God.

Condemnation is the voice of accusation. It is the lie of the devil as he articulates his indictment against mankind. The Bible declares that he stands and accuses the brethren day and night. The devil is the author of sin's allegation. We must understand that accusation is one of the primary tools used by the voice of condemnation.

Jesus Did Not Condemn

In the New Testament, there is an account of a lady caught in the act of adultery. She was thrown at the feet of Jesus by her accusers, who expected her to be stoned according to the law of Moses. However, at the end of the entire ordeal, after her accusers left, Jesus asked, *"Where are your accusers?"* Then He said, *"Neither do I accuse you, go and sin no more."*

Jesus revealed the heart of the Father in His acts of mercy, forgiveness, and remedy. The voice of condemnation that manifested through the accusations of the Pharisees demanded blood. However, Jesus manifested redemption and remedy. He said, *"He that is without sin, let him throw the first stone."* Jesus smacked the voice of condemnation in the face! His remedy was, "Go and sin no more" (John 8:11).

It is important to understand that accusations usually possess a desire to affix guilt and issue punishment. Condemnation has no interest in declaring a remedy for the issue. It strictly focuses on the violation and wants justice without mercy. It never seeks reconciliation but rather alienation. This is the goal of the voice of the accuser.

Condemnation Is Not His Nature

Condemnation is antithetical to the very nature of God. Jesus said that He did not come to condemn the world because it is uncharacteristic of His nature. The nature of God is to restore and reconcile; His nature is to declare a remedy for the problem. Contrastingly, the voice of condemnation will only declare the problem without a remedy.

When Jesus spoke with the woman at the well in Samaria, He told her she was living a sinful lifestyle. He said she was shacked up with someone to whom she was not married. However, He never condemned her. Instead, Jesus used her to ignite a revival in the city of Samaria. Is that not amazing?

The voice of condemnation will scream that you sinned and are unworthy of God's blessing. The voice of the Lord will declare you are righteous by faith in His blood and the power of His resurrection. The voice of condemnation will shout that you will never be used by the Lord because of your past. The voice of the Lord will declare you are anointed to bring deliverance to those who are bound.

Identity Based Upon Your Past

The primary goals of the voice of condemnation are to separate man from the promises of God, produce a sense of unworthiness, rob them of their confidence in God, and steal destiny and purpose. It uses accusations, rejection, and projected guilt in attempts to enforce these things. It seeks to make people believe that they are rejected rather than accepted, guilty rather than forgiven, and defective rather than restored. These are the lies that the voice of condemnation speaks in an attempt to accomplish its goals.

The enemy desires to establish an identity within you based on your past sins and failures. The voice of condemnation will remind you of the areas where you stumbled and fell. This is the enemy's attempt to shame you into receiving an identity contrary to who you are in Christ. If he can convince any believer that they are someone other than who God says they are, he can deceive them and rob them of their inheritance.

We should recognize these thoughts as the voice of the devil and then take them captive with the authority of God's Word. We must rise up with our weapons of warfare and cast down every vain imagination that attempts to exalt itself above the knowledge of God. You can say, *"Let God be true and every voice of condemnation a liar!"*

Forgiveness and Acceptance

Think about this. If God commands us to forgive others, it is unreasonable to think He would not do the same. If God commands us to be gracious to one another, it would be hypocritical for Him not to do the same. God does not command us to refrain from judging and condemning others while He engages in the act of condemnation. God's nature is remedy, restoration, reconciliation, and redemption.

Condemnation always seeks to lock people out. It desires to seal the door shut and disallow the imperfect. The voice of the Lord says, *"Whosoever will, let him come and drink."* **One of the most amazing attributes of the kingdom of God is not who it keeps out but who it lets in.**

God is not trying to keep people out; the door is open to all who desire. It is condemnation that seeks to lock people outside while looking through the window at others enjoying the blessing of the Lord. What better way to make someone feel like an unworthy and rejected second-class citizen? This wicked voice lies to people by saying that everyone received an invitation to the party but them. Condemnation desires to separate and alienate believers from the very kingdom where they belong.

God's Word declares that we are accepted in the beloved. It also says that we are no longer strangers but fellow citizens of the household of God. That means we are part of God's household; I live with God in His house. Think about that in the same manner as someone in your household living under the same roof. That is what it means to be a part of the household of God!

I eat at His table, the one He has prepared for me. I am clothed with His righteousness that He tailored specifically for me. If the voice of condemnation declares there are skeletons in your closet, just remind him that there are none in the household of God. Your closet was cleaned out by Jesus when you exercised faith in the power of His blood. The only thing in your closet now is a robe of righteousness and the garment of praise. Hallelujah!

No Place for Condemnation

The voice of condemnation brings accusation, judgment, and punishment. Jesus endured the accusation, suffered the judgment, and bore our punishment at Calvary. This means that He bore it for us, and there is no need for us to bear it. If He took it, then I don't have it. Therefore, the voice of condemnation is not a legitimate voice that I should embrace. It is a voice that I should ignore and deem not worthy of hearing.

Paul said there is no condemnation to those who are in Christ Jesus (Romans 8:1), which means there is no place for the voice of condemnation in the life of a believer. As believers, we should refuse to listen to its lies. Take the sword of the Spirit and wield it against the voice of condemnation. Cut off the tongue of this wicked voice with the promises of God that are "yes" and "amen!"

God's voice speaks of who you are in Christ. He will speak of your inheritance. The Lord surrounds you with His promises that proclaim His blessing over your life. The voice of condemnation seeks to silence the voice of the Lord. Send the voice of condemnation back to hell; it has no place in your life!

Let's look again at the account of the woman taken in the act of adultery:

> Then the scribes and Pharisees brought to Him
> a woman caught in adultery. And when they
> had set her in the midst, they said to Him,
> "Teacher, this woman was caught in adultery,
> in the very act. Now Moses, in the law,

commanded us that such should be stoned. But what do You say?" This they said, testing Him, that they might have something of which to accuse Him. But Jesus stooped down and wrote on the ground with His finger, as though He did not hear. So when they continued asking Him, He raised Himself up and said to them, "He who is without sin among you, let him throw a stone at her first." And again He stooped down and wrote on the ground. Then those who heard it, being convicted by their conscience, went out one by one, beginning with the oldest even to the last. And Jesus was left alone, and the woman standing in the midst. When Jesus had raised Himself up and saw no one but the woman, He said to her, "Woman, where are those accusers of yours? Has no one condemned you?" She said, "No one, Lord." And Jesus said to her, "Neither do I condemn you; go and sin no more" (John 8:3-11).

In this account, we see two contrasting voices displayed. The voice of the scribes and Pharisees cried out for condemnation of this woman. They did not merely want the act to be condemned and correction brought; they desired condemnation, judgment, and punishment. They wanted blood.

There was no opportunity for repentance, forgiveness, or restoration. The only thing they could embrace was the need for retribution. The woman had sinned, and they believed there needed to be action taken, which involved her being stoned.

Again, there was no opportunity given for any act of redemption, and no remedy other than stoning her was even considered.

I want to point out that the voice of condemnation always eliminates and removes the chance for redemption, forgiveness, and restoration. Understand that voices seeking to merely punish and sentence someone through edicts and declarations are not the voice of Jesus. When a voice is not laced with redemption, it misses the very heart of God because that is the way His heart is bent.

Tunnel Vision That Blinds

What caused this voice of condemnation to be so ingrained within the scribes and Pharisees? While there are possibly multiple things that contributed to this condemning heart they possessed, I believe there is one primary thing which promoted it more than any other. Simply, they elevated their bent perception of the Law above mercy that was God's nature. Let me say it another way. They elevated something God said through a man (Moses) above the very heart of God. They had tunnel vision that focused on one aspect of the Law: judgment and punishment.

It would not have taken too much research for them to realize that David not only committed adultery but also had Uriah killed. David was not stoned but forgiven. Yes, there were consequences for his sin. However, God forgave and restored him. A remedy was brought to a terrible situation as mercy triumphed over judgment.

David confessed his sin. He repented of what he had done, and God extended mercy and grace to him. This demonstrated the heart of God to forgive, restore, and bring remedy rather than condemn and punish David for his sin. David demonstrated a pattern for all believers to follow, and God exhibited a pattern that would result if we would do so.

Mercy Trumps Judgment

The examples of God's mercy and forbearance are littered throughout the Bible in the books of history, the books of the kings, the book of Psalms, books of poetic writings, and the books of the prophets. Even people who were not in covenant with God were spared when they repented. The entire city of Nineveh was spared when the people repented; mercy triumphed over judgment, and the city was sustained.

The scribes and Pharisees were consumed and controlled by the voice of condemnation because they elevated and focused on the words of the man Moses rather than the demonstrations of the heart of Jehovah. Their view of the law blinded them to understanding God's attribute called mercy. They were so consumed in the religious aspect of keeping the law of Moses that they missed the very heart of God.

> "Woe to you, scribes and Pharisees, hypocrites! For you pay tithe of mint and anise and cummin, and have neglected the weightier matters of the law: justice and mercy and faith. These you ought to have done, without leaving the others undone" (Matthew 23:23).

171

The truth is that we can become involved in doing things within the kingdom of God to the point where we miss God's heart if we are not careful. We can do the right things but miss the things that are the most important. **Jesus said the Pharisees had been faithful to tithe but had missed the weightier matters that involved mercy; He indicated that mercy itself was part of the law. Think about it!**

The scribes and Pharisees had tunnel vision. They focused on one part of the law that spoke against sexual sin yet ignored the part that spoke of mercy. Let me say it another way. The Pharisees broke the law by attempting to enforce the law because their hearts were controlled by the voice of condemnation. By ignoring the weightier matter of mercy, they gave their ears over to condemnation and broke the law. Yes, the Pharisees broke the law because they ignored the more important part that involved showing mercy.

Remedy and Solution

On the other hand, Jesus looked at the woman caught in adultery after all her accusers left and said, "*I do not condemn you!*" Jesus disabled the voice of condemnation and spoke with a voice of forgiveness and restoration. He brought a remedy to the situation by telling her to discontinue her sinful lifestyle.

As Christians, we should be those promoting remedies rather than just articulating problems. I have found that those who are always talking about problems are also the ones that blame others with the voice of condemnation. Believers should live as agents of restoration, not voices of condemnation. We should be the ones who have solutions and remedies rather than echoing the problem.

When Jesus came to this earth, there was a sin problem. He did not come to echo the obvious in the ears of everyone. Instead, He came to bring a remedy to sin and its curse. Jesus paid the price for sin to be removed and grace to abound. He made a way for man to be delivered and liberated from the power of sin and experience the very life of God.

Jesus did not come to earth to point His finger in someone's face and say, "*You are the problem!*" He came to stretch out His arms on a cross and say, "*I am the solution!*" This is the difference between the voice of condemnation and the voice of salvation. Think about it!

It doesn't take a rocket scientist to articulate a problem. Anyone can condemn another for an evident mistake. But, it takes someone who has encountered the Lord to see people plagued with sin and shout, "*Mercy is greater.*"

People who allow the voice of condemnation to speak through them usually have a warped idea of the character and nature of God. They see Him as one waiting to render judgment. Their perspective is of an angry old man sitting on his front porch waiting for someone to step into his yard so He can shoot them. This sort of idea and perspective is warped by a false understanding of the God we serve. He is not looking for a reason to punish you; He's looking for a way to bless you! He desires to take the mess you made and bring a remedy, not doom you eternally.

Past, Present, and Future

The voice of condemnation always seeks to tie you to your past. However, the voice of the Lord speaks to your present and future. It speaks to where you are now and where you are going. It is important to understand that the Lord is not interested in reminding you of everything you have ever done that is wrong or sinful.

The Bible clearly refers to satan as the "accuser of the brethren." On the other hand, Jesus is referred to as our Advocate and Justifier. Satan is the one who wants you imprisoned for your past. Jesus is the One who argues on our behalf like a defense lawyer in a courtroom. The basic argument He presents is that His blood is greater than the accusation, so the case must be dismissed. Hallelujah!

There is a monumental difference between these two positions. One seeks to condemn and punish with no hope for recovery. The other seeks to forgive and extend grace with the hope of things being restored better than they were previously. Satan's voice puffs condemnation while the voice of Jesus breathes restoration.

A Saul Can Become A Paul

Before Paul became a great apostle of faith, he was Saul of Tarsus who persecuted the Church. On the road to Damascus, he experienced an encounter with Jesus. Please bear in mind that Saul had already executed Christians. He was a religious zealot who sought to squelch the spiritual insurrection in Israel called Christianity. He hunted down Christian leaders in the hope of discouraging and hindering the gospel from being preached.

When Saul (Paul) encountered Jesus, he was knocked off his horse and blinded. Jesus asked him why he was persecuting Him. When Saul asked who was speaking to him, the Lord replied, "*I am Jesus.*" Saul then asked the Lord what he should do, and Jesus gave him direction on where to go, and there he would receive instructions on what to do.

One of the things so fascinating about this story is what most Christians seem to miss. Saul had killed and was continuing to kill Christians. Yet, when Jesus shows up in his life, Saul is offered a remedy rather than judgment. He is offered redemption rather than condemnation. The voice of condemnation is nowhere to be found in this entire discourse. Jesus showed up to change Saul into Paul, not condemn Paul for the sin of a wicked Saul. Jesus brought a remedy, not retribution for Saul's sin.

Lessons for the Modern Church Culture

In the modern Church culture of today, if someone even threatens our defined Christian living, many are ready to call fire down from heaven on them. If a political leader does something that we believe violates our biblical morality, then we are ready to wage war against them. **It seems that believers often speak the language of condemnation rather than reconciliation. We become the Pharisees to the woman caught in adultery rather than Jesus, the remedy for her sin. Think about it for a moment.**

Things done in the name of taking a righteous stand must be bathed in love and clothed with a remedy. We must understand that there can be no greater righteous stand than what Jesus exemplified. He offered Paul forgiveness, redemption, and remedy rather than guilt, condemnation, and punishment. Jesus never sought to bring retribution upon the head of Saul (Paul) for killing His children. Saul did some awful things, but Jesus offered him a place in His kingdom.

Many times, believers get angry about something happening within the present culture, and then they yield to the voice of condemnation. In doing so, they unknowingly reflect the voice of the enemy rather than the voice of the Lord. Their emotional reactions to something of which they disapprove cause them to condemn others rather than seek peace and resolution.

If Jesus could forgive Saul for killing His children, then we certainly should be able to forgive others. Likewise, if Jesus told the woman who was caught in adultery that He did not condemn her, then we certainly should be able to say the same to our lost neighbors and extend a hand of mercy to them.

Saul killed believers, but Jesus saved him and gave him a ministry. Perhaps we would not be so quick to condemn and judge others if we considered they might be one that God uses to minister to others in the future. The Saul of Tarsus today may be the apostle Paul tomorrow.

A Righteous Stand Doesn't Require Condemnation

It is good to take a stand for righteousness, but it is not right to become the voice of condemnation. It is good to articulate a biblical moral standard that God has declared, but it is wrong to pass judgment on those who do not ascribe to the same.

The voice of condemnation will always seek to target individuals and people groups. The voice of righteousness will seek to target the destructive sinful conduct. We must be able to separate the sin from the sinner because that is what Jesus did. He separated the act of adultery from the woman who was caught doing it. Jesus separated the sin of murder from the man called to be a great apostle and write half of the New Testament. He separated the sinful lifestyle of a woman with five husbands who was living with another man from the woman He would use to bring revival to an entire city.

This is what redemption is all about; it separates us from our sin. Jesus became the remedy so that sin would no longer be attached to us. That is why Paul said, "There is therefore now NO CONDEMNATION to those who are in Christ Jesus" (Romans 8:1, emphasis added). You have been separated from condemnation, and it has no right to attach itself to you any longer. Therefore, I am not going to allow the voice of condemnation to be released in my life or through my mouth!

If you are saved, you are free from condemnation. The voice of condemnation has no power or authority within your life. Your record has been erased and replaced by the very blood of Jesus and His righteousness. Remember, Jesus did not come into the world to condemn it (the sinners and lawbreakers); He came so the world could be saved and set free from sin and condemnation. Rejoice!

VOICES 2

12

ANGELS & DEMONS

> But to which of the angels has He ever said: "Sit at My right hand, Till I make Your enemies Your footstool"? Are they not all ministering spirits sent forth to minister for those who will inherit salvation? (Hebrews 1:13-14).

It is essential for us to recognize that angels have an important role in the earth. They also have a unique ministry that they serve in the lives of believers today. Although we have dealt primarily with voices of deception within this book, the voice of angels dispatched from the Lord are not sent to deceive. On the other hand, the voice of demons comes specifically for that purpose. Therefore, I wanted to include some basic understanding concerning the voices of angels and demons.

Throughout the Bible, we observe the manifestation of angels. Angels were used to speak to human beings on earth, delivering messages from heaven to men and women. While most people will never have an angelic visitation, we need to realize that angels are real and have a voice to speak.

Angels are spirit beings that dwell in the spirit realm. Unless God opens our eyes to see into that realm, they are invisible to us. However, we see numerous times in Scripture where God allowed people to see angels.

Angels Echo God's Voice

Angels do God's bidding by harkening to and obeying His voice. They echo what God is saying. Angels always speak in accordance and agreement with what God is declaring, which means that any legitimate angelic proclamation will always agree with the Bible. Just as accurate prophetic words agree with the words of Jesus, so will any legitimate angelic voice or visitation.

Throughout the Old and New Testaments, we witness the manifestation of angels. The word "angel" literally means *a messenger with the primary purpose of delivering divine messages.* They are dispatched as servants of God to convey heavenly assignments and communications. They function as divine servants who do the Lord's bidding as they harken to the voice of His Word.

Angels are not purposed by the Lord to destroy relationships, eradicate people from our lives, and bring edicts without redemption. That is **not** the role of angels. Instead, they come to reinforce the very things that Jesus came to accomplish. Jesus came to save, heal, and deliver. Therefore, the voice of angels will echo and declare the same things for those to whom they are sent and dispatched. They do not function independently of the voice of the Lord.

First Mention of Angels

The first mention of the angel of the Lord in the Bible involves delivering a message to Hagar, the servant of Abraham's wife, Sarai. This angelic appearance happens on the heels of Hagar running away after Sarai dealt harshly with her. The angel instructed Hagar to return to Sarai and submit under her hand. The message delivered to Haggar was one of reconciliation and reuniting.

It is interesting to note that the first mention of the voice of angels in the Bible reveals the very heart of Jesus. His desire is reconciliation, restoration, and recovery. It is important to realize that legitimate manifestations of angels point people toward being reconciled to God, their fellow man, and the purpose of God for their lives.

This is a crucial understanding to possess concerning angels. In theological studies, the law of first mention establishes that the biblical introduction of anything becomes the foundation for its existence. Since the first mention of angels has to do with fostering reconciliation, we must conclude that this is a foundational element of their ministry. The voice of angels comes to restore and revitalize. Their primary purpose is **not** the destruction and annihilation of people or relationships. Failure to understand these things can cause people to discern angelic voices and visitations improperly.

Even in the account of Lot living in Sodom, the angel of the Lord was sent to deliver him from destruction. The angels did not come to deliver a message of destruction but rather to rescue Lot and his family from being destroyed. There is a remarkable difference between the two.

Angels will reinforce what Jesus has spoken in the same way God established the voice of prophecy to do the same. Angels will be in total agreement with everything that Jesus taught, demonstrated, and accomplished through His redemptive and substitutionary acts. Angels echo what Jesus said and is saying. They speak the same message.

Ministering Spirits for the Heirs of Salvation

Angels are ministering spirits sent to those who are heirs of salvation (Hebrews 1:14). We can observe angels ministering to Jesus after the devil tempted Him. They obviously possess a vital role in the earth since Jesus received their ministry. It is not clearly stated how the angels ministered to Jesus, but we know they did.

God commissions angels for different tasks. We know they protect those who are in covenant with the Lord. They bring deliverance as they did with Lot and his family. While on a ship battered in a storm, the apostle Paul said the angel of the Lord appeared to him and brought assurance that no lives would be lost. This is the dimension of protection and safety that angels bring.

We observe angels revealing to Mary and Joseph about the supernatural birth of Jesus. Then they proclaimed His advent to shepherds and gave them directions to where He was located. The primary visible role of angels we see in the New Testament is that they deliver messages to God's people.

There are people I have known who claim to have seen angels. Numerous people in our church body have claimed to see angels in our church building. I have never seen one, but I certainly do not doubt that their testimony is true. Angels are real, and they minister to those who are the heirs of salvation.

Afforded Angelic Protection

Many people think of angels as only a means and source of protection and safety. We have all heard the phrase "guardian angel." It is used in relation to the thought that God has assigned an angel to us for the purpose of protecting us from danger. This idea is derived from Psalm 34:7, which declares that the angel of the Lord camps all around those who fear Him, and He delivers them.

While I believe that God protects us and His angels are near us, the idea of a specific guardian angel assigned to us individually cannot be fully supported by Scripture. That appears to be more of a Hollywood invention rather than a Bible principle. However, that does not discount God's protection within our lives or that His angels are around us.

The angel of the Lord is not to be compared with what is seen in the movie *Angels in the Outfield*, which helps you catch baseballs that are uncatchable. We cannot allow movies to dictate our perception of the ministry of angels. The only thing that should frame our perception of the ministry of angels is the written Word of God. If we do not possess an unshakable standard to evaluate supernatural manifestations, we will be led into error by inaccurate interpretations and fabrications.

> But even if we, or an angel from heaven, preach
> any other gospel to you than what we have

preached to you, let him be accursed. As we have said before, so now I say again, if anyone preaches any other gospel to you than what you have received, let him be accursed (Galatians 1:8-9).

These are powerful words uttered by Paul. He specifically said that any angelic message which proclaimed any other gospel different from what he was preaching should be accursed. The word "accursed" means *banned*. In other words, it should be considered illegitimate—false and unworthy to be believed or followed. It should be regarded as nonsense!

He went further to say that any person who came preaching a different gospel than what he preached, let him be accursed. Paul was not playing around. He was serious about maintaining purity in doctrine. He commanded supernatural experiences to be scrutinized and spiritually discerned as to their accuracy.

Real Experience but Illegitimate Message

Paul clearly indicated that every prophetic revelation, whether acquired through an angelic visitation or heard from a pulpit, should be judged and evaluated by the measuring tool of the gospel he was preaching. If it were contrary in spirit and content to what he had declared, it would be discarded and considered fallacious.

The apostle Paul commanded the Church to judge all voices of supernatural revelations regardless of the source. The experience that fostered the revelation was not to be considered, while the content of the word was to be judged. I recognize that this is not a popular idea in some prophetic camps, particularly those prone to embrace sensational manifestations. However, failure to do so is missing the mark and will ultimately lead people down the path of deception.

Someone can have a real experience yet hear something false and illegitimate. The encounter alone does not make the message true. Heaven can open, and a host of angels ascend and descend, but if their message is contrary to the gospel, it must be considered false. The truth is not determined in the experience but rather in the message that is delivered. This is the reason that Paul gives parameters for evaluating angelic voices and visitations.

The bottom line is that if anyone has a supernatural experience, but the message is contrary to biblical teaching and principle, it must be judged as nonsense. Regardless of the validity of the experience, it must be evaluated according to the content of the message.

It would require an entire book to discuss what angels say and do fully, but the purpose of this chapter is not to accomplish an exhaustive study of the ministry of angels. The primary thing I desire to focus on is that the voice of angels is a legitimate source from where God will articulate messages for man. He has created angels for that purpose, and they will speak harmoniously with the words of Jesus.

The Voice of Demons

> Then they came to the other side of the sea, to the country of the Gadarenes. And when He had come out of the boat, immediately there

met Him out of the tombs a man with an unclean spirit, who had his dwelling among the tombs; and no one could bind him, not even with chains, because he had often been bound with shackles and chains. And the chains had been pulled apart by him, and the shackles broken in pieces; neither could anyone tame him. And always, night and day, he was in the mountains and in the tombs, crying out and cutting himself with stones. When he saw Jesus from afar, he ran and worshiped Him. And he cried out with a loud voice and said, "What have I to do with You, Jesus, Son of the Most High God? I implore You by God that You do not torment me." For He said to him, "Come out of the man, unclean spirit!" Then He asked him, "What is your name?" And he answered, saying, "My name is Legion; for we are many." Also he begged Him earnestly that He would not send them out of the country. Now a large herd of swine was feeding there near the mountains. So all the demons begged Him, saying, "Send us to the swine, that we may enter them." And at once Jesus gave them permission. Then the unclean spirits went out and entered the swine (there were about two thousand); and the herd ran violently down the steep place into the sea, and drowned in the sea (Mark 5:1-13).

Just as I said concerning angels, it would equally require an entire book to do an exhaustive study on demons. There are some wonderful books that speak to this subject completely. I want to primarily focus on the fact that just as angels speak and deliver messages from the Lord, demons speak and deliver messages from satan.

Demons are spirit beings. They operate in the realm of the spirit. However, they manifest in the natural realm through human beings. Demons will speak lies and false information to bring destruction to humans. Those who heed their voice will ultimately be destroyed.

In the previous Scripture, we see a demon speaking through a possessed man, and Jesus confronted and talked to it. Jesus did not carry on a dialogue with an imaginary being, but He cast the demon out of the maniac of Gadara, and the man was delivered. So, demons are real entities that operate in the spirit realm yet manifest in the earthly realm.

Demons Have a Voice

It is important to note that demons have a voice. They will speak to people and tell them to harm themselves and others. For example, this demon spirit told the man to cut himself; it told him to run around naked and live in a cave. The voice of this demon motivated the man to engage in self-destructive behavior.

Demons will speak to people to do things that are harmful. They seek to control someone's life for the purpose of tormenting and destroying them. They are the agents of hell on assignment to steal, kill, and destroy. This is the mission they desire to accomplish.

We can see how demons foster and promote self-mutilation. This kind of manifestation results from people listening to the voice of demons. Engaging in various forms of cutting is a form of self-hate that is common among those who give heed to demonic voices.

I believe some of the piercings that people allow in their bodies are forms of mutilation. These are things that believers should avoid. It is one thing to have an unnoticeable piercing for an earring. It is yet another thing when that piercing becomes a complete mutilation of your body parts. I do not say this to condemn anyone but to encourage people not to do it. Our bodies are the temple of the Holy Spirit and should not be mutilated.

Demons Work with the Flesh

Demons will also work in conjunction with the flesh, particularly when the voice of the flesh is heeded. Fleshly and sinful behavior opens the door for demonic spirits to infiltrate the lives of men and women. They take advantage of the opportunity to establish strongholds in people's lives. This hellish grasp is empowered and reinforced through their voice that utters lies and untruths.

It is important to note that demons speak the same thing internally to the ones they inhabit as what you hear the person say audibly. An unclean spirit will speak unclean things internally to those it occupies, and then they will speak and manifest unclean things to those who can observe it. A lying spirit will lie to the ones they possess and to the ones who listen to the possessed person. Demons manifest through people externally the same thing it speaks to them internally. Demons are consistent liars.

The man we read about earlier, known as the maniac of Gadara, was possessed by a spirit named Legion, actually numerous demons. The man was moved to do vile things such as dwell naked in the caves, engage in acts of mutilation, and shout out obscenities and threats to those who passed by. He was totally controlled by demonic spirits and heeded their instruction 24/7.

The controlling voice in this man's life was the voice of demons. It motivated him to harm himself and threaten the safety of others. He conducted his life in an uncivil manner which was a nuisance to those forced to see him. The demons inside convinced him to behave in inappropriate ways that were vile by every definition.

The voices screaming in his internal ears were most likely deafening. He was tormented day and night by demonic verbal instruction that led him to a place of insanity; he literally lost his mind.

Obscenity and the Demonic

As a rule, when people behave in an obscene manner, it is because they are listening to demonic voices. Unnatural and uncontrollable behaviors are typically indicators of demonic control within the individual's life. Usually, the voices of demons have gained control of the people who conduct their lives in these manners.

Those who engage in obscene activity, whether it is spoken out of their mouths or the actions of their bodies, are typically listening to the voice of demons. Demonic voices motivate this vile behavior. Those who possess what we call "potty mouths" usually are controlled by demonic voices. They hear demons speak and then repeat it like parrots.

It is ungodly to speak with continual obscenities coming from your mouth. Any person who claims to be a Christian that consistently uses obscene language needs a trip to the altar where they can receive deliverance from the demonic voices they are heeding. Believers should not give themselves over to this type of influence. Close the door on the voice of demons by filling your mouth with God's Word rather than hell's garbage.

Just as Jesus cast out demons, we must do the same. Their harassing voice is silenced when they are cast out. The demon-possessed man tormented by the legion of demons was restored to his right mind after he was delivered. The voices could no longer torture him or motivate him to hurt himself.

Demons Desire Destruction

When Jesus cast these demons into a herd of swine, they ran down the hill into the sea and drowned themselves. What these demons could not accomplish in a man because of Jesus' intervention was fulfilled in animals; they destroyed the herd of pigs.

We can observe the goal of the voice of demons as demonstrated. They are enlisted in the army of satan and do their master's bidding. The devil's command is to destroy everything accessible. So, anywhere they have access, they seek to destroy.

Demonic entities have a voice. The language they speak is falsehood. They have no ability to tell the truth; they can only lie. Their master is satan, and they echo the monologue of hell. Their voices seek to do one primary thing: destroy God's creation. They desire to pervert and destroy everything that God created but especially mankind. Their purpose received from the devil is to reflect and enforce pain, suffering, and death.

We Have Authority

Fortunately, we have power over demons. Jesus said we can cast them out in His name. He said that we have power to tread on serpents and scorpions and over all the power of the enemy (Luke 10:19). We have been commissioned to silence the voice of demons, and we should take our weapons of warfare and shut his mouth. Refuse to allow the voice of demons to reign in your life.

As Christians, we have been given authority over all the power of the enemy. This means we can silence every demonic voice that seeks to kill and destroy. Take authority today over every voice of deception that the enemy may attempt to use to ensnare you. Arise in the power of the Holy Spirit and crush the head of the enemy with your weapons of spiritual warfare. Silence the enemy with the Word of God and your praise. Jesus is Lord, you are an overcomer, and the devil is a liar!

You need not be deceived by the voice of the enemy. We are filled with the wisdom of God and have been given the keys to the kingdom. So, let us arise as children of the light and refrain from heeding the voices of darkness. We are the sheep of His pasture, and we follow the voice of the Good Shepherd!

VOICES 2

13

Let's Get It Right

Many other voices could be further discussed in this writing; the voices of deception are plenteous. They seem to be everywhere today. In our modern internet and social media culture, someone only needs an electronic device and a personal page to promote anything they so desire. Unfortunately, this has given way to a deluge of deceiving voices present in the world today.

Less than 40 years ago, much of this was not possible. The accessibility for any person to be given a free platform to promote any foolish thing was not available. However, it is now fully obtainable to anyone.

This is the reason we must learn to discern the voices we hear. Everything must be measured by the standard of God's Word, the Bible. It is the measuring stick that we use for everything we hear. Failing to know and use God's Word will result in Christians ultimately falling prey to deception, just as Eve did in the Garden of Eden.

The Root of Biblical Ignorance

Biblical ignorance is a significant problem in the world and the Church today. Over a decade ago, a survey was conducted that polled professing Christians. Here are some of the astounding results:

- Less than 50% of Christian adults can name the four Gospels
- Over 50% of believers cannot identify more than three of Jesus' disciples
- 60% of Americans cannot name five of the Ten Commandments
- 81% of believers in America believe that the saying "God helps those who help themselves" is a verse in the Bible
- Over 50% of adults believe that the Bible teaches the single most important purpose in life is to take care of your family
- 12% of Christian adults believe that Joan of Arc was Noah's wife
- Over 50% of high school seniors believe that Sodom and Gomorrah were husband and wife
- A considerable amount of people believed that the Sermon on the Mount was preached by Billy Graham
- Theology students entering college did not know the difference between Saul in the New Testament and King Saul in the Old Testament—and some actually believed that Joshua was the son of a nun (rather than knowing that Nun was the name of his father)
- Only about a third of Americans read their Bible at least once a week

Reading some of these results can initially cause one to chuckle a bit. However, when the gravity of the situation hits, it will cause a concerned person to weep. Biblical illiteracy is a real problem the Church faces today.

Sadly, this issue is not going away anytime soon. It will require a revival of biblical knowledge to take place for it to be corrected. This means that pastors and leaders within the Church will need to become more concerned about imparting understanding and wisdom than entertaining a gathering with a fifteen-minute pep talk on Sunday mornings. It means that families, dads and moms with their children, will need to make an intentional effort to be in their local church when the doors are open. It means that convenient Christianity will have to be replaced with committed Christians.

Bible Knowledge Comes through Study

We cannot expect anyone to know the Bible if they do not hear it, read it, and study it. There is no way that someone anointed by God can lay hands upon a person and impart biblical knowledge. It comes in one way only: consistent study.

Think about this for a moment. We send our kids to school five days a week to be in one-hour classes to be taught six different subjects. They spend five hours a week in a math class plus additional homework. **So, in math alone, our kids spend an average of 8-10 hours a week. Yet, these same children, on average, spend maybe 1-2 hours a week at church if they are faithful. Think about it.**

This is the reason we have these issues today. This is what contributes to many believers falling prey to the voices of deception. Many Christians are biblically illiterate and therefore have no measuring stick for what they are hearing.

Discernment begins with biblical knowledge. From there, it proceeds with spiritual training that sharpens your spiritual senses to know good from evil. However, the Bible is the basis from which all of this evolves. Without it, we will miss it and mistake something bad for what is good. While Bible knowledge alone is not the cure for the spiritual discernment problem present within the Church today, we will surely be deceived without it.

Look Inside Again

As stated earlier, I believe God is calling for the Church to take an introspective look. He desires to give us eyes to see so that we will not believe a lie and fall into the snare of the enemy. We must be willing to look at ourselves and measure everything we believe. If it fails to pass evaluation of the Word and Spirit, we must eliminate it. If we post things on social media that are not sure to be the truth, we must refrain from continuing to do so (and possibly remove some things). If prophets are speaking things inaccurately, then it needs to be judged as such, and changes need to be implemented.

None of this is meant to condemn anyone. Instead, it is said to encourage us to repent and change if we are going in the wrong direction. Correct what needs to be corrected, and let's move forward with truth and accuracy. If things were said in our zeal that proved to be wrong, fix it and press ahead with a determination never to make the same mistake again.

Danger in Defensiveness

Becoming defensive over mistakes benefits no one, and it does harm to the Church. Unfortunately, some ministers are more interested in saving face and their reputation than doing what is right to edify and build up the Church. This manifestation of pride is the same thing that caused the downfall of individuals throughout history, starting with Lucifer. His pride ultimately caused him to lose his call, anointing, and ministry. My friend, it is not worth it!

The time for doubling down on error is over. It is essential to realize that true humility is needed for the prophetic ministry to be accurate and maintain its integrity. Accuracy begins with the understanding that anyone can miss it. This one understanding will help ministers and prophets remain humble more than anything else.

The moment anyone thinks or believes they are infallible is the moment that falling is imminent. For one to think it impossible to speak or prophesy something inaccurately starts them down the road of destruction. Historically, all major false teachings within the Church were born out of the belief that it was inerrant and could not be questioned. The promoters doubled down on their declaration when challenged by those with knowledge of the Word. Rather than taking an introspective look, they embraced an attitude that defied anyone who contested their proclamations. This kind of conduct has resulted in many people being hurt.

Likewise, defensiveness over a word prophesied is usually the badge of error. It is the declaration of infallibility and unwillingness to be evaluated. This attitude leads to greater error and multiplied inaccuracies.

One Lie, Two Lies

One of the things that I was taught growing up was always to tell the truth. It was drilled into me that honesty is the best policy. My parents and leaders in the Church warned me that one lie would lead to another. Once someone tells a lie, they must continue to lie to cover up the first lie. One untruthful statement causes someone to reproduce and multiply more untruths.

This same principle applies to inaccurate prophetic words or declarations. When it is coupled with defensiveness, it only reproduces more inaccuracy. When a prophecy doesn't materialize, the voice of human reasoning will give reasons that are often merely the voice of fleshly justification. One inaccuracy unchecked gives way to other false things declared. It becomes a destructive deception snowball rolling down the hill called error. It will roll on and capture more people with it until someone is willing to admit their fallibility and mistake.

Go Low

Any person that believes God has called them to be a prophet must rid themselves of defensiveness. Any individual who believes they have a prophetic gift must allow evaluation of that which they speak. They must adopt an attitude of meekness and teachableness. Pride and haughtiness will always go before a fall and destruction. Above all things, anyone gifted to prophesy must embrace a spirit of humility. It is the only way someone will successfully make it to the end of their race here on earth.

I have seen instructional fire training for those who might get caught inside a burning building. When smoke fills the place, breathing becomes impossible as it rises to the top. The instruction I have seen repeatedly is to "go low." In a smoke-filled room, any oxygen in the room will be near the floor.

Staying low is the only way to survive in these types of situations.

Using this analogy, in a world full of inaccurate voices (smoke-filled room), it is imperative that we remain humble (go low) so that we come out on the other side unscathed. If we attempt to lift ourselves up, we will suffocate. However, if we "go low," we will overcome and live. We must remain humble and allow what we speak to be evaluated, particularly when it comes to prophetic declarations involving current events. Doing this will enable us to survive the smoke and continue down the right road.

Agreement Does Not Mean Accuracy

It is important to realize that people shouting words of agreement with your prophetic declaration at a conference does not make it truthful. Thousands of people liking a post on social media does not mean it is accurate. A congregation getting excited about what is being said does not guarantee that it is right. Likewise, playing to the crowd that agrees with your statement does not mean it is the truth.

I have seen people post things that are biblically inaccurate and get multiple thousands of likes and shares. On the other hand, I have seen people post things that are in perfect agreement with the Bible and have nothing but hateful comments of disagreement. The number of people echoing what you say or post never determines its accuracy.

Unfortunately, social media has both developed and exposed in many Christians a longing for man's approval. The reality is that all of us want people to like what we are saying; we all desire approval. However, acceptance of our statements on social media platforms never guarantees that it is correct. It only reveals one thing—people like it. **Just remember this, the Israelites in the wilderness loved the golden calf. Think about it!**

If we state things that resonate with someone who has idols in their heart, they will love it and give you a wholehearted "amen!" Things that reinforce an idol will not be rejected or challenged. Rather, it will be received and applauded. When people hear what they want to hear, it will be embraced without any thought given. When people hear what they don't want to hear, it will be met with disapproval and skepticism. The bottom line is this: Agreement does not equate to accuracy, and disagreement does not equate to inaccuracy.

Accountability Is Not Rejection

As was said earlier in this writing, the prophetic ministry is an important God-ordained ministry in the body of Christ. God placed prophets in the Church to strengthen and develop the body of Christ. The Church cannot fulfill everything that Jesus desires to be brought forth without the functioning of this vital ministry. It is imperative that we continue to embrace what Jesus placed within His Church. Although there has been error spoken by some prophets, we should not throw the baby out with the bathwater.

However, the need for accountability is an issue that we cannot ignore. It is particularly necessary in our social media age, where anyone can have a platform and claim to be a prophet. Anything can be said and have the name of the Lord ascribed to it. Unfortunately, we have seen that most of these words declared by Facebook prophets rarely materialize, and there is no accountability that they embrace. This development has led to a deluge of "prophetic words" articulated on social media platforms by those with no voices of evaluation in their lives or ministries.

Greater power always requires greater parameters. For example, someone can take a 9-volt battery and touch it to their tongue. They may experience a slight surge of electrical power, but it will not be enough to do them harm. However, I cannot allow wires to hang down in our church building flowing with 220 volts of electricity. If someone grabs hold of it, they will die. The principle we see demonstrated is that the greater the power, the greater the need for parameters to flow properly and safely. Without proper measures in place, that which is purposed to bring life will produce death. Something good can become something destructive if it is void of proper parameters. Likewise, the more anointed that someone believes they are, the more accountability they need within their life.

Things Needed for Prophetic People

Here are just a few important things that need to be present within a person who believes they have any type of prophetic gifting.

First, they need to be planted in a local church with a local church pastor. If you are going to have a voice, then you need a pastor. Everyone needs a spiritual shepherd in their lives. I recognize that Jesus is the Great Shepherd. However, there are representatives that He has placed on earth called pastors who lead and feed the sheep. They are tasked and anointed for that purpose. Failure to receive from a spiritual shepherd can result in people going the wrong direction and listening to wrong voices.

Secondly, they should operate in a spirit of humility, allowing their prophetic words to be evaluated. I have told our local church body, "If you don't want your prophetic word to be evaluated, then remain silent." That is not meant to intimidate anyone from prophesying. Instead, it is said to let everyone know there are measures of accountability in place for the protection of those within the church.

Thirdly, they must be willing to admit mistakes pointed out to them by reliable voices of accountability, especially when it is obvious. Saying that you missed it does not mean you are weak. It is not the badge of a heretic but rather the badge of the humble. When there is something very specific prophesied that does not materialize, we should at least be willing to examine it closely and admit to any mistake. Doing this is a good thing.

Fourthly, they should be students of the Word. People prophesy in proportion to their faith. They will speak out of the well that they already possess inside of them. If they are consumed with false doctrine or teaching, their prophetic ministry will usually reflect it. An anointing to prophesy does not replace or erase biblical ignorance or false doctrine. Therefore, it is crucial for those who prophesy to know their Bible, particularly New Testament principles governing the operation of the prophetic ministry within the Church.

> And the spirits of the prophets are subject to the prophets. For God is not the author of confusion but of peace, as in all the churches of the saints (1 Corinthians 14:32-33).

Any prophetic voice within the body of Christ should recognize that they are responsible for what they speak. The Holy Spirit does not force people to utter anything. No one can blame God for confusion born out of their prophetic word. Therefore, accepting responsibility for things uttered falls in the laps of those who speak it.

Since the spirit of the prophet is subject to them, we must understand that they must accept responsibility for what they utter in the name of the Lord. If a prophetic word is bringing confusion to the body of Christ, then it should be honestly evaluated. If correction or adjustment is needed, the prophet (or prophetic believer) should gladly acknowledge it and take proper actions. To refuse to evaluate and make needed adjustments is failure on the part of the prophet.

Rejection of correction is worse than a false or presumptuous prophecy. **An inaccurate prophetic word can be given from a sincere heart that hears incorrectly, whereas rejection of correction is born out of pride. Think about it!**

Confusion will always be the byproduct of things spoken presumptuously or from a wrong spirit. The voice of truth will never be bitter or vindictive; it will not seek revenge or retribution. God is not the author of confusion but peace. The voice of the Lord does not seek to destroy but rather to build and bless.

Pain, Bitterness, and Judgment

We must be cautious that we do not convolute our own experience and God's nature. I have witnessed ministers go through tragic and heartbreaking events within their lives.

From there, they established their own belief system based upon their interpretation of the tragedy through human rationale. Since the emotional pain was so great, they construed their feelings and saw their experience through the lens of God's plan for their life. Unfortunately, this rationalization caused them to make incorrect assumptions concerning the character and nature of God.

Instead of seeing God as a loving Father who desires good things for His children, they saw a God that sends pain and catastrophic situations to help teach us what we need to learn. Instead of seeing God as a Redeemer who is rich in mercy, they saw Him as the God of judgment and retribution, just waiting for the right moment to pour out His wrath. As a result, their glimpse of the Lord became skewed and off-kilter. This resulted in their prophetic words being tainted by the incorrect assumption they made about the very nature of God.

The general line of thinking is that if this horrible thing happened to me (God's servant), then it must undoubtedly be the will of God. Therefore, it must be something that everyone should experience. This line of thinking is nothing more than an attempt to put a spiritual spin on something that happened to them because of living in a fallen world where we also contend with the demonic forces of hell. God had nothing to do with their pain and suffering. Their experience was never a reflection of the character and nature of God.

Many of these ministers end up prophesying out of a well filled with bitterness. They are bitter toward the world, the church, and even God. Ultimately, they begin to prophesy how God is bringing judgment and calamity to the world. They may even name areas of the nation or the world that will be struck by God's wrath and displeasure.

Going back to the aforementioned Scripture, God is not the author of confusion BUT OF PEACE! God does not desire confusion and calamity; His will is peace and blessing! He has a good plan for His people; He desires that His good will be fulfilled within all of us. This is the reason that Jesus came to Earth!

The Voice of Light

During one of the darkest moments of history, when the Roman Empire had control of Israel, Jesus arrived on this planet in Bethlehem as a baby in a manger. The Roman Empire was filled with every kind of evil and sin imaginable. There was idolatry, prostitution, slavery, and barbarism, just to name a few. So, what does God do in the middle of great darkness prevailing in the nation of Israel? He sends the Light; He sends Jesus.

When Jesus was born into the earth, the angels proclaimed, "Glory to God in the highest, and on earth PEACE, GOOD WILL toward men" (Luke 2:14, emphasis added). They did not proclaim, *"Ah, you did it, and now you're gonna get it."* The angelic proclamation was one of redemption and goodness. It was a declaration that light had come into the world to dispel darkness. In this dark time, the proclamation of redemption was being made; it was not a declaration of judgment and punishment.

Understand that God did not send the Light into the world to make it darker. He released light to dispel the darkness. Jesus was not sent into the world to cause it to be more sinful; rather, He came so the world would be freed of sin. Jesus came to erase what satan brought into the world. He came to turn back the clock and return man back in the place from which Adam fell! Hallelujah!

At the beginning of all creation, we read that God stepped out into the middle of darkness. He did not curse or judge it. Instead, He released the antithesis of the problem with His VOICE. He said, "Let there be light." God did not make commentary on the darkness; He spoke His desire and will!

It seems today we have many who refer to themselves as prophetic yet only want to make commentary on the darkness that is apparent. They seem to take the news headlines and turn them into something prophetic. It does not take an anointing to do that; things which are out of order are obvious. However, a man or woman of faith is required to boldly speak God's will and desire in the face of the craziness of our world today.

Echo Jesus

I believe God is still stepping out into the darkness and releasing His voice with the proclamation of light. The power of His redemption is greater than the power of sin, and this truth continues to echo throughout the earth. His voice will destroy and annihilate every voice of hell and bring things into His divine order. Therefore, we must tune our spirits to His voice and echo what He is saying today.

Jesus is declaring life where there is death. He is declaring health where there is sickness. He is declaring restoration where there is destruction. He is declaring righteousness where there is sin. This is what God is saying because that is His will and plan for our lives. Anything short of this gives us reason to question if what we are hearing or declaring is accurate.

We must stay in step with the words and actions of Jesus. If you want to know what God is saying today, look at Jesus. Read the words He spoke while walking upon this earth. Look at the manner and way in which He conducted His life. See your neighbor and your enemy through the eyes of redemption and salvation. Doing this will enable us to discern the voices of deception and embrace the word of the Lord. Let the life of Jesus be the measuring tool we use today to discern what is truth and what is deception.

My prayer for you is that God will cause you to be keen in the spirit. I pray that you will be able to discern between what is good, bad, and godly. Finally, I pray that no voice of deception will influence you in any area of your life and that you will be led by the voice of the Good Shepherd.

May God anoint our ears to hear clearly and our mouths to speak accurately and precisely. In Jesus' name, Amen!

THINK ABOUT IT POINTS

Take a moment to consider these points:

- Eve was deceived because she thought the voice of the thief was actually the voice of a friend (ch 1).
- It is impossible to properly discern the voices you hear if you do not know the Word of God (ch 1).
- People are susceptible to voices of deception when they have an itch they want to have scratched (ch 1).
- The voice of justification will cause someone to believe something is right that is actually wrong (ch 3)
- Heeding the voice of offense causes believers to forfeit God's blessing within their lives (ch 4).
- The root of rebellion is often found in giving place to the voice of offense (ch 4).
- Our voice can become a channel for deception if we exalt our opinions and personal desires above God's Word (ch 5).
- When someone's heart becomes polluted, they fail to discern properly—they believe they are right when they are obviously wrong (ch 6).

- A believer's heart can become contaminated by ministers who have polluted wells (ch 6).
- David's strong desire to build the house of the Lord became an exalted thing in his life. Even a good thing can become an idol in someone's heart if improperly discerned (ch 7).
- When Jesus was on trial, the Jews cried, "We have no king but Caesar." Loyalty to a political power caused them to miss their Messiah (ch 7).
- Unrighteous leaders are the ones that need the most prayer—we don't only pray for the righteous (ch 10).
- Jesus indicated that the practice of showing mercy was a part of the law that should be obeyed (ch 11).
- Jesus did not come to earth to point His finger in someone's face and say, "*You are the problem!*" Instead, he came to stretch out His arms on a cross and say, "*I am the solution!*" This is the difference between the voice of condemnation and the voice of salvation (ch 11).
- Often, believers speak the language of condemnation rather than reconciliation. We become the Pharisees to the woman caught in adultery rather than Jesus, the remedy for her sin (ch 11).
- An inaccurate prophetic word can be birthed from a sincere heart that hears incorrectly. However, rejection of correction is born out of pride (ch 13).

ABOUT THE AUTHOR

DR. ROBERT GAY is Senior Pastor and Apostolic founder of High Praise Worship Center in Panama City, Florida. His ministry has a three-fold vision statement: Equipping Believers, Building Families, and Furthering the kingdom of God. Robert provides apostolic oversight to multiple High Praise churches within the United States. He is recognized by many as a prophetic and apostolic voice bringing balance and order into the church today. For complete bio, go to www.highpraisepc.com.

Silencing The Enemy With Praise
Pastor Robert Gay

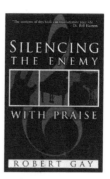

Praise and worship are more than words and music says author Pastor Robert Gay. Praise is a weapon of warfare. God will fight for you as you praise the greatness of His name.

"The contents of this book can revolutionize your life...It brings new understanding about the power of praise and worship."
-Dr. Bill Hamon

Planted
Pastor Robert Gay

Robert Gay confronts common "church issues" head on. He teaches with clarity and compassion that God is the Master Gardener who lovingly tends to every individual planted in His garden. You will find out how God wants to plant you so that you will flourish and grow and become everything He wants you to be.

"Every Pastor will appreciate this book...every saint of God should read this book..." - Dr. Bill Hamon

Best Of Robert Gay
Pastor Robert Gay

This compilation album represents some of Robert's most impactful songs that have touched the body of Christ throughout the world. This cd is packed full with 19 tracks that include powerful songs such as Mighty Man of War, Lord Sabaoth, On Bended Knee, Holy is Your Name, One Voice, No Other Name and much more!

Sonship
Pastor Joshua Gay

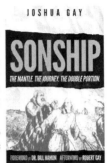

Discover the life of a true son through study of the Scripture and powerful testimonies. The author shines the light on many pitfalls that ensnare today's generation while revealing the true picture of faithful spiritual sons and daughters.

"This book needs to be read by every person who wants to be a true son or father according to God's order." - Dr. Bill Hamon

Faith Force Academy LIVE DVD
Volume 1: Meet The Faith Force

Join the Faith Force Heroes and Professors M & C in *Faith Force Academy LIVE!* as they teach you how to become strong superheroes of faith! This volume contains 4 exciting episodes that kids of all ages will be sure to enjoy. Each episode features exciting praise & worship, step by step teaching of scripture memory verses, incredible life-sized characters, & illustrated sermons.

Faith Force Academy LIVE DVD
Volume 2: Faith Is The Victory

Join the Faith Force Heroes and Professors M & C in *Faith Force Academy LIVE!* as they teach you how faith is our victory! This volume contains 4 exciting episodes that kids of all ages will be sure to enjoy. Each episode features exciting praise & worship, step by step teaching of scripture memory verses, incredible life-sized characters, & illustrated sermons.

Jesus In 3D
Pastor Robert Gay

Do you want to express the life of God in every aspect of your life? In your ministry? For us to walk in the totality of Jesus, we must first cherish the fullness of His ministry. Every dimension of the ministry of Jesus is critical for us to have ultimate effectiveness for the kingdom of God. Today, if you want to reflect the life of God, you must receive and activate all that He did, everything He said, and everything He demonstrated.

Revolutionaires
Pastor Joshua Gay

Revolutionaries declares to readers that God is raising up a transformation generation in the earth today. Discover the life of a spiritual revolutionary through the study of scripture and parallels from history.

"...if you read this book you are going to be enlightened, motivated and activated into being one of God's "Revolutionaries." - Dr. Bill Hamon

Building Strong
Pastor Robert Gay

There is a blueprint that the Father has rendered for the design of the Church. Jesus has been given the responsibility of building what was in the mind of the Father from creation. The Holy Spirit is the agent that empowers and gifts the spiritual subcontractors here on earth to build according to the plan that has been rendered from heaven.

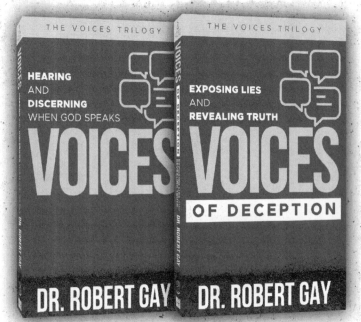

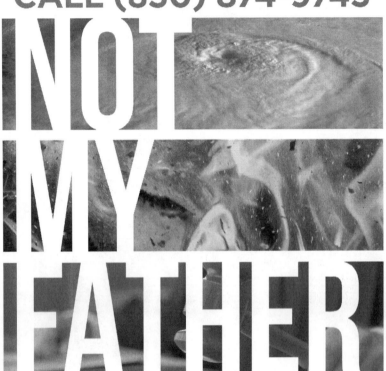

NOT MY FATHER

UNDERSTANDING GOD'S NATURE IN THE MIDST OF
STORMS, DISASTERS, AND JUDGMENT

ROBERT GAY

219